Interred Within

The Pioneers of Guysborough

Publisher - Guysborough Historical Society

CONTENTS

Forward

by Duncan Floyd, K.C. (From a 1921 copy of the *Canso Breeze*)

Last Sunday afternoon I spent a few hours in the cemetery of Christ Church, Guysboro, poring over old inscriptions on tombstones below which "the forefathers of the hamlet sleep." This is one of the oldest grave yards in the Province and I was saddened to see its dilapidated condition. Many of the old tombstones are down and grown over with grass and turf, others still standing are covered with moss. In one case "Time's effacing fingers" had completely obliterated the inscription. In one place, about the centre of the cemetery, was a place newly ploughed. A desecrating mind had conceived the idea of levelling off the place with a plow and the vandal hand that carried out the conception did it to his mentor's liking. As I gazed on the evidences of neglect of those who have made "the pilgrimage of the unreturning feet," I wondered if the public could be stirred up to undertake the work of restoration.

I looked in vain for many tombstones that I knew were once there. I saw at one grave a stone tumbled over and had difficulty in getting any part of the inscription. This was over the grave of a man who for nearly a century filled a large place in our early history, the Hon. Robert M. Cutler. From his grave I looked across to the old French graveyard on the Stearns' place (approximately adjacent to where the swimming pool is by he highschool), not more than five hundred yards away. Across the harbour I could see the grove of trees in whose shadow sleep the first old settlers. I thought as I looked, of the tragedies that had been witnessed here, the sorrows, the misty eyes that had looked out in times past down old Chedabucto: for the old graveyard has seen nothing of joy but much of sorrow. I thought of the trials of those old pioneers, the hardships encountered, the fortitude with which they bore them. Their struggle against hunger and privation, their labour in clearing away the virgin forest, the fewness of their pleasure, the multitude of their anxieties. And all for what? For ideals. For the privilege of living their lives in their own good way, of making a free home for posterity. What brave men and women. Can one conceive of heroism more worthy of admiration than that of the pioneer? Without hope of fame, devoid of the incentive of public approbation they suffered and endured, toiling on faithfully to the end.

I was constrained to admit that we do not "Hold high the torch flung" from the long decayed hands of those brave men and women who "Loved and were loved" in the long ago, else we would cherish the sacred spot where they lie. As I slowly rubbed the moss from the inscription or removed the turf, I reflected on the ingratitude which could permit such a condition of affairs to continue.

This cemetery should be attended to at once. In a few years it will be too late. Under intelligent supervision the old stones could be exhumed and set up properly, the slabs which once rested on pedestals could be restored, the moss on the stones still standing could be removed and the lettering on many now becoming illegible, could be renewed. Can we find enough citizens of our town to restore this old spot to something approaching respectability? And more important still can we find some person or persons with means who will contribute towards this good work. I am sure the *Breeze* would accept contributions towards this very desirable end.

The condition of this lot is the highest tribute that could be paid to the descendants of the McColls who live at New Glasgow and who some years ago paid a sum of money to put this lot in order. Their noble example is worthy of emulation.

Introduction

by Jamie Grant

The region of which Guysborough is a part was one of the first in North America to be both contacted and later settled by Europeans. The identity of the first European to glimpse this area is anybody's guess, with Saint Brendan, various Norse adventurers, Prince Henry Sinclair, Basque fishermen, John Cabot, Jean Cartier et al having been nominated for the honour at one time or the other. Whenever it occurred it was very early. Captain Johann Deneys had a map of the area published in Paris in 1508, the Baron DeLeary reportedly left cattle at Canso in 1518 and Captain Savalette made his first fishing trip here in 1564.

The French under Sir Isaac de Razilly made the first successful attempt at permanent settlement in 1632 with the establishment of a fishing and fur trading post at the mouth of Guysborough Harbour named Fort St. François à Canso. The Canso Acadians maintained a presence here for 133 years, not withdrawing until France surrendered North America to Great Britain in 1763. Their place was soon taken by New England *Planters* who then shared possession of it with the Mi'kmaw. This was until May 16th, 1784 when the first of more than 1,100 Loyalists arrived marking the birth of Guysborough as we know it today. The old Yankee families suddenly found themselves engulfed by a sea of new comers who must have been one of the most diverse groups to ever descend on a remote pioneer community. Almost a quarter were black, mainly former slaves with some still in bondage. Race was hardly all that separated them. They were also divided by class, religion, language, nationality, ethnicity, regimental loyalties, etc. However, their common need to survive forced mutual cooperation and a degree of tolerance unusual at the time.

That same year, 1784, Sydney County (Antigonish and Guysborough Counties today), was established with Guysborough designated as shire town and local government established. At its first session, October 11, 1785 a motion was passed to ask Governor John Parr's assistance in procuring a clergyman. Their desires were met in the person of Rev. Peter De la Roche whose arrival on July 23, 1786 marked the beginning of Christ Church Parish.

His burial of the infant Ann Farfer in 1787 like wise gave birth to Christ Church Cemetery.

For the next thirty years the rectors of the parish provided Christian funerals and burials to all regardless of sect or race. This ceased with the establishment of Roman Catholic, Methodist, Baptist and Presbyterian churches. Perhaps this explains the uncommon degree of interdenominational goodwill which seemed for the most part to prevail. There are many examples of this: such as Charlotte Newton's Sunday School attended by all denominations. As well, William Desson, a Catholic, donated one of his town lots adjacent to Christ Church Cemetery for its enlargement. Thomas Cutler's (Anglican) pro bone procurement of the land for St. Anne's Catholic Church and glebe house and H. M. Jost's (Methodist) provision of a bell for St. Patrick's Chapel, all attest to the ecumenical spirit of the community.

Today Christ Church Cemetery, with its mingled bones of various sects, classes and races, is a physical testament to the community's early diversity and inclusiveness, values now considered the essence of the Canadian identity.

The Christ Church Cemetery Project

"... these bones from insult to protect.
Some frail memorial still erected nigh
... Implores the passing tribute of a sigh ..."
Thomas Gray

The genesis of this book was a joint project of the Anglican Parish of All Saints by the Sea and the Guysborough Historical Society. It was intended to restore Christ Church Cemetery and to erect commemorative panels naming those buried within. These dual aims were to address the neglected state of the burial ground and reveal the anonymity of most of the pioneers interred there without tombstones. It was agreed that the parish would fundraise while the Society would research, design and erect the panels, and lead in the restoration of the cemetery.

The Society's interest stemmed from it considering Christ Church Cemetery the pioneer graveyard of the area. The Mi'kmaq certainly buried many in unknown sites and the French are known to have had two cemeteries here before their removal in 1764. However, we have no idea who is buried in them and only a vague idea of their locations. It is also true that a few of the earliest English pioneers were buried in a private graveyard on the old Hadley property on the Manchester side of the harbour before the establishment of a church. Christ Church Cemetery however is the fist true cemetery of the Guysborough we know of, begun in 1787 and with the last burial occurring in 1938. For much of its long existence it was poorly maintained.

Its history of neglect is well documented. Charles Buckley recounted that while a student in the 1890's he and his companions could hide from the view of their teachers in the overgrown bushes of the cemetery. Thirty years later, in an impassioned plea written in the *Canso Breeze* in 1921 (see Forward), D. Floyd admonished the community for allowing "one of the oldest cemeteries in the Province" to fall into such a shameful condition. Perhaps his challenge was accepted by some, for the tombstones of Robert M Cutler, the De La Roches and others he mentioned as either down or derelict, have since been stood up. None-the-less the cemetery continued to be over grown and with gravestones fallen over.

In the early 1950's a flock of goats breached the churchyard fence and made considerable headway against the impenetrable tangle of wild roses, laurels and withrods which had long since taken over. Though they were expelled from the cemetery, their example seemed to have inspired human action. A new fence was erected and some of the fieldstones, which had marked the place of many burials, were removed, facilitating the mowing of some portions of the cemetery. Much of the labour involved was supplied by prisoners of the Guysborough jail under the supervision of the high sheriff or jailer.

Eventually death and out migration reduced the congregation of Christ Church past the tipping point. The church was inactivated and the cemetery again took on the look of neglect.

It was at this point that the fore mentioned project was begun. The fund raising exceeded expectations and costs kept to a minimum thanks to volunteer labour and donated materials and machine use. The chief difficulty faced was the presence of a number of large dead trees, some of which threatened the church, utility lines and tombstones. These were expertly removed by a local lumberman/entrepreneur at no cost. The other trees, some over sixty feet high, were removed by the Guysborough Historical Society volunteers and the brush burned. Several tombstones were found under the turf and re-erected as were some badly broken stones which were epoxied back together.

Compiling the names of those buried within the cemetery proved much more challenging than anticipated. First, there seems to have never been a burial plot plan and over the years most of the fieldstones which marked grave sites had been removed. Also a number of broken tombstones had been placed on the stone walls which defines the southern and western boundaries of the churchyard. Most of the inscriptions on these were indecipherable. All of this made it virtually impossible to determine the burial layout pattern, or if there had ever been one.

The official burial records, of which scanned copies were provided by the Anglican Diocesan Archives, also presented unforseen difficulties. First, they contained obvious gaps suggesting either the loss of some portions of the record or the failure of the rector to make the entries. For example, no deaths were recorded from 1798 to the end of 1803 while sixteen were noted in 1804. Most of the early records don't specify the place of internment making it virtually impossible to know if those who died far from town were buried in the cemetery or on their own properties. In such cases all that could be done was to decide what was most probable. But, sometimes the improbable is the reality, as in the case of young Nelson Ballaine. He was the son and grandson of prominent Anglicans who lived about a mile from the cemetery and nothing in the record suggests he was buried elsewhere than the cemetery. However, the presence of his tombstone on family property proves there can be no safe assumptions. It is almost certain there are other instances of what seemed most likely being not what actually occurred.

There was also a marked variation in the quality of the records kept by the different rectors. Rev. De La Roche, the fist rector, recorded full names, ages and in most cases, the cause of death. By contrast, his next two successors, J. W. Weeks and his son Charles Weeks, seemed to place a low priority on record keeping. Entries such as, "aged black woman", "Anderson, very old" and "unknown woman" provide few clues to the identity of these people. The quality of Charles Weeks' handwriting was an added difficulty. As well, there are tombstones which were erected during this period which contain names not entered in the burial records. So poor was the record keeping done by the Weeks, not even the burial of the Senior Weeks by his son was recorded! The records from this period are sorely wanting.

Considering all of the above it's obvious that there are many interred in Christ Church Cemetery of whom there is no record. There are others not properly identified. So it must be acknowledged that the list of 764 names on the commemorative plaques is incomplete and is not without errors.

The completion of the project was marked by a celebratory service in Christ Church followed by the unveiling of the commemorative panels. The event ended with a reception at the Old Court House Museum where food abounded and good cheer shared.

In retrospect the success of the project exceeded its aims. Not only was the cemetery restored, but thanks to the generosity of the donors, its continued maintenance is assured well into the future. The church building, the third on the site, will likely disappear in the not too distant future but the cemetery will remain, a rare physical bond with our pioneers. The panels will serve to strengthen that connection.

This book is another outcome of the project. As work in the cemetery progressed, volunteers shared what little each knew about those "interred within." In 1897 Guysborough historian H. C. Hart wrote, "Guysboro has had many residents in bygone days whose names and characteristics should be preserved." The biographies which follow attempt to do just that.

Daniel Aikens 1787 - 1870

by Mark Haynes

Born on April 25, 1787 in Greenock, Scotland (just west of Glasgow on the Clyde), Daniel Aikens (also spelled Aiken or Atkins), joined the Royal Navy sometime before his 17th birthday.[1] He is most noted for being a member of the crew of HMS *Temeraire* at the Battle of Trafalgar in 1805. Under the command of Captain Eliab Harvey, the *Temeraire* was the second ship in Admiral Nelson's column to make contact with the Franco-Spanish fleet. When Admiral Nelson's HMS *Victory* came in danger of being boarded from the French ship *Redoutable*, the *Temeraire* was brought about and discharged a double-shotted broadside into the enemy ship. The action was described by Captain Jean Jacques Lucas of the *Redoutable*:

> The three-decker [Temeraire] ran afoul of the Redoutable to starboard and overwhelmed us with point-blank fire of all her guns. It would be impossible to describe the horrible carnage produced by the murderous broadside of this ship. More than two hundred of our brave lads were killed or wounded by it.[2]

Temeraire then rammed the *Redoutable* and poured continuous cannon fire into her. At the same time the 112 gun Spanish ship *Santa Ana* and the 74 gun French ship *Fougueux* came up on the *Temeraire's* un-engaged starboard side. She was now fighting three enemy ships at the same time.

---

[1]In the Ayshford Trafalgar Roll there is a James Aikens from Greenock listed as an Able Bodied Seaman from Greenock, Scotland, who was at Trafalgar. It is suspected this is the same person. Perhaps his full name was James Daniel Aikens and he preferred his middle name.

[2] Warwick, Peter, *Voices From the Battle of Trafalgar*, Newton Abbot: David & Charles, 2005, pp. 200-1.

Captain Harvey later commented to his wife:

> *Perhaps never was a ship so circumstanced as mine, to have for more than three hours two of the enemy's line of battle ships lashed to her.*[3]

Redoutable, sandwiched between the British ships *Victory* and *Temeraire*, was reduced to a floating wreck with 300 dead and 222 wounded. In risk of sinking, Captain Lucas called for quarter and surrendered to Captain Harvey. Despite being sandwiched between two enemy vessels, Captain Harvey dispatched a boarding party who entered one of the enemy ships through her gun ports. The French fought the ensuing attackers below decks port by port until their captain, Louis Alexis Baudoin, was killed. At this point the ship surrendered.

Admiral Horatio Nelson in the thick of it, Trafalgar, 1805.

By this time the *Temeraire* had fought both French ships to a standstill and had suffered 47 killed and 76 wounded in the process. Eight feet of her starboard hull was smashed in and all her sails and yards had been

---

[3] Willis, Sam *The Fighting Temeraire* London Querous, 2010, p. 193

destroyed, leaving only the lower part of her masts still standing. *Temeraire* then came under fire from a counter-attack by the as-yet unengaged van of the combined Franco-Spanish fleet, led by Rear Admiral Pierre Dummoir le Pelley. Captain Harvey ordered what few guns which could still be fired brought to bare with the attack eventually beaten off.

HMS *Temeraire* survived the battle and a storm the next day which caused the death of another 47 of her crew. She eventually limped back into Portsmouth on December 1, 1805. In total she suffered 170 casualties in the Battle of Trafalgar. She became famous in British lore as the ship which saw the most action, not only at the Battle of Trafalgar, but in the history of the British Navy. Her image was enshrined forever in a painting by J. W. Turner "The Fighting Temeraire tugged to her last berth to be broken up, 1838". It was voted Britain's most favourite painting in 2005.

Young Daniel must have experienced a very interesting day at Trafalgar. In all likelihood he would have been a gunner during the battle as all hands would be needed for this task. His normal position on the ship when it was not in combat is listed in naval records as an Able Bodied Seaman. Having learned the art of war from the world's best naval tactician, he served aboard a Halifax privateer capturing American ships during the war of 1812. It is thought he made enough money from his share of the prizes to purchase property at Crow Harbour (Queensport), Guysborough County in 1816 and settle down.

On December 19, 1814, he married Charity Jamieson. They had children John (1815), Jane (1818), Robert (1821), Charlotte (1825), James (1827), Marianne (1830), Margaret (1833) and Daniel (1836). In the census of 1838 he is listed as being a cooper. There is not much else known about Daniel from the date he settled in Guysborough until his death on May 7, 1870 and internment in Christ Church Cemetery. Perhaps he preferred a quieter life after all the adventure. Hats of to Daniel Aikens!

Original entry of the internment of Daniel Aikens in Christ Church records.

The Fighting Temeraire tugged to her last berth to be broken up, 1838, by J. W. Turner (National Gallery)

Ab Bayard 1753 – 1810

by Chris Cook

Amongst the several lists of Loyalist setters in Harriet Hart's book *History of the County of Guysborough*, is one titled *Negroes at Chedabucto*. The name Ab Bayard appears on this particular list. Bayard (now spelled Byard), came to Guysborough with the classification "Free Black". Little is known about Ab, likely Abraham, after his settlement in Guysborough except for his date of death and subsequent burial in Christ Church. However, thanks to the extensive work done by Nova Scotian historian, Stephen Davidson, we do know generally what Ab went through to earn his freedom, and eventually settle here in Guysborough. Davidson is also a leading expert on the content of the well-known *Book of Negroes*. He writes:

> *A remarkable ledger lists all of the Africans who left the Thirteen Colonies through the port of New York City in 1783, and in that record we can discover the names of some of the Black Loyalists who served the crown as wagon drivers. The Book of Negroes recorded four ships as departing New York in the fall of 1783 with passengers who had once served in the Wagon Master General Department. The Peggy, Nisbet, Elijah, and Joseph took their loyal evacuees to settle along the coast of Nova Scotia between Shelburne and Liverpool. Some African teamsters made Port L'Hebert their new home, but most settled in Port Mouton.*

It is highly likely that Ab Bayard was one of the Black Teamster who landed at Port Mouton; the original Guysborough. He left New York City, November 9, 1783, on the ship *Nisbet*. From the *Book of Negroes* we know that Ab Bayard was described as, "30, stout fellow. Formerly slave to Samuel Bayard, Cecil County, Maryland; left him in 1777."

Samuel Bayard died in December of 1776, just after the outbreak of the American Revolution. Ab Bayard probably saw this as the perfect opportunity for freedom. If Ab joined the British forces as an avenue to escape the USA, it means he served the entire duration of the war. Davidson describes how diverse a group the Black teamster members were. He writes:

> The Black Loyalists who served the crown as teamsters hailed from all over the Thirteen Colonies: South Carolina, Rhode Island, Pennsylvania, Virginia, New Jersey, New York, Massachusetts, Delaware, and Maryland. The British needed wagon drivers whose knowledge of the roadways and geography of the colonies would allow them to choose the fastest and safest routes to strategic locations. Being aware of the places these Black Loyalists were once enslaved also provides clues as to where they served as teamsters. The diversity of colonial origins for the Black Loyalists also demonstrates what an amazing variety of people settled the rocky coasts of Nova Scotia in 1783. The fact that they could unite and form new communities in such an inhospitable climate is a testimony to their determination to overcome differences in background and culture.

The reality of the surname Bayard is that it is not Ab's family name. As he was forced to take the name of his slave owner, we may never know his true family identity. Interestingly, Samuel Bayard had a son named Peter Bayard; and from the Christ Church records, it is known that there was a burial of a Peter Bayard here in 1827. Were Ab and Peter connected? It would seem unlikely that their presence in Guysborough at this time was a random coincidence.

Escaped slaves like Ab Bayard would do whatever necessary to be free from their past lives. Willingly signing up to be teamsters, enduring the horrors of war with its likelihood of death, and then a voyage in the cold Atlantic waters on the verge of winter to our rugged shores; paled in comparison to the alternative. The present day descendants of Ab Bayard have much to be proud of in their ancestor. The bravery it took to start a new life in Guysborough as a refugee is something few of us will ever truly understand.

Conestoga Wagon, typical of those operated by the Black
Teamsters during the American Revolution: 1776 - 1783

Daniel Bigsby (Bixby) 1723 - 1788

by Jamie Grant

Almost two and a half centuries have passed since the Rev. Peter De la Roche wrote the only known local reference to this man vis. "Daniel Bigsby frozen to death on Birch Island 19 February, 1788 aged 65". Another entry in the church record, dated 7 May, 1791, records the baptism of Catherine, born 1778 and Sarah, born 1781, daughters of Mrs. Catherine Bigsby. Family lore maintains that these two girls were born at the Guysborough Intervale. As scant as these records are, it has been possible to peal back some of the mystery surrounding this old pioneer.

Some time in 1938, Reverend A. W. Eaton examined the records in Guysborough and Halifax while others consulted records in New England. Rev. Eaton also recorded the family lore from several great grandchildren who resided in Guysborough at that time. Combining the information from these sources it can safely be concluded that Daniel Bixby was born in Chalmsford, Middlesex, Massachusetts in 1723 and that he married Catherine Spaulding in Connecticut and that they had a son named John. Some confusion results from the family's insistence that Daniel, "had came from Connecticut", but records from that state proved he was not born there. The solution seems to be that he and Catherine lived there before departing for Guysborough.

Tradition also holds they first lived at the Intervale and latter moved to Guysborough. There is a deed for two acres in Manchester being sold on the 19 November, 1788, by Mansfield Munson to Catherine Bigsby "of Boylston", so perhaps it was to there they moved from the Intervale. Daniel's descendants also knew how he had died. He had gone shooting ducks on Birch Island (the larger of the two islands in Guysborough Harbour), and his boat drifted off with the tide when he wasn't looking, leaving him to freeze to death.

The remaining mystery is when did the Bigsbys come to Guysborough and under what circumstances? It has been suggested he may have been a seasonal fisherman who decided to live close to the fishing grounds year round, but this seems unlikely considering his age. Also, it seems unlikely that a veteran fisherman would neglect to tie his boat on a rising tide close to a channel with a considerable current. If he indeed had lived at the Intervale, he was likely a farmer and the mistake that led to his death would be more understandably made by a landsman. There is definite proof that Benjamin Hallowell of Boston was bargaining with "a number of families to settle on his 20,000 acre land grant and that several had travelled there in 1773 to assess prospects. Might Daniel Bigsby have been one of them? Hallowell had been run out of Boston by the rebellion and went to London and so was not in a position to conduct business in Nova Scotia, and, at the Intervale, there were the recently abandoned Acadian farms which meant cleared land. Perhaps Bigsby squatted on one of these only to be evicted when the whole area was granted to the Loyalists. At this point we simply don't know when or why he came and can only speculate.

However, though Daniel Bigsby's life here was shadowy, the name he brought to the area has been preserved through his son John's eight sons and by Bigsby's Head in Cook's Cove and Bigsby's Brook in Guysborough.

James Bowie 1750 - 1836

by Mark Haynes

James Bowie's original British Army discharge papers were found in the attic of his home in Havendale, just outside of Boylston, in 1979. They show he was from Paisley (Abbey), Scotland. Genealogical research on both Ancestors.com and My Heritage, Library Edition web sites show he was born on March 25, 1750, to parents Alan Bowie and Ann Smith. He was christened on March 27 at Paisley Abbey. Raised in the Presbyterian faith, it was essential to be able to read in order to interpret the bible for oneself and hence he was literate. Due to this requirement, Paisley, headquarters of the Presbyterian church, to this day is home to the oldest literary college in Great Britain.

By the age of twenty-six he had become a blacksmith. In 1777 he joined the 76th Regiment of Foot, MacDonald's Highlanders, also known as the Immortals, who were raised that year for participation in the American Revolutionary War.[4] His uncle, John Bowie Sr., had already emigrated to the American colonies in 1705 at the age of seventeen. John Bowie Sr.'s son, John Bowie Jr. (James Bowie of Guysborough's 1st cousin), and grandson Rezin Bowie (James Bowie of Guysborough's 2nd cousin), threw their hats in with the rebels and as a result James Bowie had relatives on the opposing side of the American Revolution.

The 76th was not shipped off immediately but instead saw home duty. Due to the promise of booty when they joined up, the regiment took part in the Burntisland mutiny of March, 1779, because of lack of involvement in the war. When MacDonald himself showed up to sort things out, the soldiers were paid and promised to see action. As a result they embarked for New York in August, 1779. They first engaged in battle at the Siege of Charleston, March to May of 1780 where American and French forces were defeated. There is

---

[4] This information comes from his original discharge papers found in 1979 in the attic of his old home in Havendale, N.S., copy of which is in the N.S. Archives.

mention in military records of James Bowie repairing wagon wheels at this time as part of his blacksmith duties.[5]

The second encounter they had with the enemy was at the Battle of Green Spring on July 6, 1781, where they charged and defeated a French American force attacking them under the command of the Marquis de la Fayette. The Americans lost all their cannons with over three hundred men killed. The 76th was then ordered to mount up, something they had never done before, and ride after the retreating Marion's Raiders, lead by the famous "Swamp Fox," Lt. Francis Marion. Unknown to James Bowie, his 2nd cousin, Rezin Bowie, was a member of this unit. To the relief of the family, Rezin, who had been wounded at the Storming of Savanah the previous year, was convalescing at the time of this encounter due to wounds and not present on the battlefield.[6] The incident is thought to be what is behind an old poem found in the attic of James Bowie's house in Guysborough, Nova Scotia, in 1979. It refers to a rift in the family over the revolutionary war which is hesitantly being forgiven;

> Add but your stripes and golden stars
> To brave St. Georges cross
> And never dream of mutal wars
> You dances dances mutal loss;
> Let us to bless when other's ban
> And love when other's hate
> And so my cordial Jonathan*
> We'll fit I calculate[7]

* Jonathan is a nickname used at the time for an American colonist originating

---

[5] Ancestors.com, Healey/Meagher/Hacket family trees.

[6] Rezin Bowie recovered from his wounds and married the girl who nursed him back to health. They had sons Rezin Jr. and James who gained fame for inventing the Bowie knife and being a colonel in the Texas revolt of 1836.

[7] Miss Maggie Long's copybook

from Britain.

Despite their efforts, the 76th never caught up with Lieutenant Marion who gave his pursuers the slip. Those dam Yankees!

James Bowie surrendered, along with the rest of the 76th Regiment of Foot, at the Siege of Yorktown in October, 1781. Rather than return to Scotland with the regiment, he took up the offer of land in the colony of Nova Scotia and left from New York in 1783 arriving at Guysborough in 1784. Financially he was better off than most loyalists as he not only received his soldiers pay of 7 shillings while in the army but also payment over and above that for blacksmith work done on a piecemeal basis.

He was given a town lot which today is undeveloped and lies adjacent to the RCMP building. He also received a lot on the north side of the Guysborough Intervale and a wood lot at some distance to the rear, a typical allotment for all disbanded soldiers. His neighbour was one William Desson, described only as an Englishman. James was not a farmer though and realized there was money to be made from the sale of lumber in the form of ton timber to the UK, now that timber imports from the American colonies were banned. This led him to sell his Intervale lot (which by then was a combination of at least 5 lots purchased from departing soldiers) and purchase of lots 80, 81, 82, 83 and 84 on the south side of the river at Havendale. Following him in the endeavour was his buddy William Desson. He purchased most of these lots for around £4 each with their previous owners taking whatever money they could get for them and catching the first ship back to the UK, Boston or Halifax. Without the wealth to invest in oxen, sleds, axes, saws and hired hands, there was little chance of their getting in on the timber trade. In other words it takes money to make money. These waterside lots were preferable over inland wood lots due to the convenience of being able to use the waterway to float logs to market.

Another reason for his wanting to locate to the south side of the Milford Haven River was the announcement in 1788 of a road to be built from Guysborough to Antigonish. Initially it was thought that it would go along the south shore of the inlet as far as the Intervale and then follow the Roman Valley inland. He was a blacksmith and wanted to be located on a road. It did eventually take this route but not until around the mid 1840's. To save money it was decided the first leg of the new road would be by water to the Intervale and then overland from there. So to a certain extent he was misled in his reason for relocating.

A house and barn (still standing and thought to be one of the oldest barns in Nova Scotia), were built here in 1788. While the post and beam structure would have come from wood on his own property, in all likelihood the cut boards for closing the structure in would have been floated down the Milford Haven River from a nearby mill on Fraser's Creek. A mill existed here during the French period and it is thought it was refurbished and used by a Loyalist entrepreneur. He married Margaret Desson, a Catholic (spelled Deason in Catholic records), on November 28, 1789. She was the daughter of William Desson indicating they had formed what was known then as a family compact. They went on to have children William 1790, Isabella 1792, James Jr. 1794 and George Sr. in 1797. In a booklet titled "Economic Opportunities at Milford Haven"[8] written between 1764 and 1784 by James Lodge, first High Sherif of Guysborough, the blacksmith skills of James Bowie is emphasized to make fittings for the construction of ships. In fact James Bowie was instrumental in the building of the ships *Peggy* in 1817 and the *Guysboro* in 1827. In the Assessment Roll - Guysborough and Manchester 1st July, 1792, his taxable income is listed at £40 - 5 shillings, placing him amongst the top twenty five wealthiest people of Guysborough.[9]

According to "King" Cutler's store ledger,[10] in 1823 at the age of seventy-three James Bowie came into his store at Cutler's Cove in Guysborough and purchased tobacco and a small amount of rum. This shows he smoked a clay pipe and wasn't a teetotaller. He also purchased sail twine and tar indicating he owned a boat. This would be essential for anyone living along the Milford Haven River. Later in the year he returned and purchased a new pair of shoes for fifteen shillings.

Also about this time a white girl, who's name is not being revealed for

[8] Copy in the N. S. Archives

[9] H. C. Hart *History of the County of Guysborough*, Mika Publishing, Belleville, ON 1975, p. 232.

[10] Guysborough Historic Society asset #148, Account Book of Thomas Cutler 1823-25

reasons of privacy, was placed into apprenticeship by her parents at the Bowie household. She was to learn the "science and mysteries of housewifery." She was forbidden to say her master's name in vain, fornicate or use cards. She was allowed to milk the cow and use the spinning wheel for her own purposes only on Sundays. Her bondage was to be served until "the Lord calleth Mrs. Bowie unto him."[11] Though St. Ann burial records are missing from 1839 to 1866, it is thought Mrs. Bowie died around 1842 and was interred in the Catholic cemetery in Guysborough.

James Bowie died on March 2, 1836 at the ripe old age of eighty-five. Coincidentally, four days later on March 6, his 3rd cousin Col. James Bowie, died at the Alamo, San Antonio, Texas during a revolt against Mexican authority. James Bowie of Guysborough was buried in Christ Church cemetery on March 4 while his relative's remains were burned three days later on March 7 in a mass cremation just outside of the walls of the Alamo.

A cairn was built to commemorate James Bowie of Guysborough at his homestead at Havendale. In the 1930's, while their parents were away at church, the eldest Bowie daughter, who stayed home to babysit her younger siblings, told them to tear down the crumbling cairn in front of the house for something to do. She recalled the children finding some kind of leather satchel, medals, tartan cloth and a red jacket, obviously James Bowie's military dress uniform from the Revolutionary War. Unfortunately all the medals were lost with there being no surviving British Army records telling what they were for.

His son William drowned in 1811 while his daughter Isabella married first James Bears in 1813 and second Donald (Daniel) Sellers in 1826 . James Jr. married Elizabeth Crescine in 1826 and was living in Antigonish by 1836 where he remained the rest of his life. George Sr., who inherited the farm, married Margaret Desson in 1827. The farm remains in the family to the present day.

---

[11] This information comes from his original bondage document found in 1979 in the attic of his old home in Havendale, N.S., copy of which is in the N.S. Archives.

Jim Bowie's barn circa 1788 (photo taken in 2017).

House built by James Bowie at Havendale in 1788 (Photo taken in 1897).

Joshua Caldwell   1810 - 1831

by Jamie Grant

Its largely forgotten that Guysborough was for many years a significant port and shipbuilding centre. Regular packet service began in the 1820's and lasted until 1955. In 1867 there were 64 ships registered here of which about two-thirds were locally built. The port was also frequented by ships from many other parts of the world, usually by choice but sometimes by chance. An incident of the latter explains how the remains of Joshua Caldwell happen to be resting in an unmarked grave in Christ Church cemetery.

Harriet Hart, that faithful recorder of local events, tells all we know about him:

> Late in the Autumn of 1830, a large vessel in charge of Capt. Baker, bound to Montreal from the Mediterranean, mistook Chedabucto Bay for the Strait of Canso, and went ashore near the entrance of Guysboro Harbor. She was floated, and came in to Mr. Cutler's wharf where she remained during the winter. Very little damage was sustained. The cargo consisted of wine, nuts and raisins. A young man named Caldwell, a passenger, was very ill and died during the winter.

There must have been many who shared his fate since life at sea was perilous and medical care primitive even when it was available.

Dr. William Russell Cantrell   1792 - 1838

by Mark Haynes

Dr. Cantrell was one of Guysborough's early medical practitioners. Born in Waterford, Ireland in 1792, he graduated from Trinity College in Dublin as a medical doctor in 1818 and became a Member of the Royal College of Surgeons. After practising there for one year, he came to Halifax in 1819, motivated partly by necessity since eloping with Mary, the daughter of his incensed Irish neighbour. He was a wealthy landowner who objected to their relationship on account of his daughter's young age.[12] After running off together, they boarded the first available ship to the colonies. It was a successful match for it is reported they remained married for their natural lives and had three children, Eliza b. 1818, Edward b. 1819 and Marianne b. 1825. The descendants of his family later lived in Truro.

According to the Acadian Recorder, he opened a Pharmaceutical and Chemical Laboratory on Barrington Street on July 10 of that year. In 1821 he moved to Guysborough where he joined Dr. Henry Inch who had been practising here since 1817. On the murder of Dr. Inch in 1829, he became Guysborough's sole doctor. One of Dr. Cantrell's more interesting medical duties occurred in 1823 when he was paid £4 from the Court of Sessions for holding an inquest into the death of George Lamb. It was his finding that the person in question had been murdered which resulted in charges being laid.

In 1827 there was an outbreak of smallpox in Sydney due to the arrival of the immigration ship Harmony. Then in the same year another immigration ship, the Stephen Wright, brought another forty passengers who were also infected with smallpox. As a result of these outbreaks, the provincial secretary appointed Dr. Cantrell as Health Officer for the Port of Sydney in 1827. He hardly took up the new position when another ship, the Two Sisters, arrived from Greenock, Scotland, in 1828 also infested with the disease. Dr. Cantrell's two year stay in Sydney turned out to be a very busy time for him considering

---

[12] A.C. Jost, Scrapbook IV, GHS, p. 82

2,473 people emigrated from Scotland to Cape Breton in this year. In 1827 while living in Sydney, his daughter Marianne died at age 13 months.

In 1829 he and his family moved back to Guysborough. Another disease scare occurred in 1834 when the schooner *Dolphin*, of Arichat, arrived from Quebec where an outbreak of Cholera had occurred. She sailed as far as Prince Edward Island accompanying the *John Wallace* of Guysborough. When the disease ran rampant throughout the crew of the *John Wallace*, the *Dolphin* broke off and sailed on to Guysborough alone. Dr. Cantrell would have recognized the symptoms of cholera only too well. It first starts with a odd sense of unease, accompanied by a slightly upset stomach. The initial symptoms themselves would be entirely indistinguishable from a mild case of food poisoning. Vomiting would shortly occur followed by muscle spasms and sharp abdominal pains. At some point the victim would be overcome by a crushing thirst. The experience is largely dominated by one hideous process: vast quantities of water being evacuated from the bowels, strangely absent of smell and colour, harbouring only tiny white particles. Clinicians of the day dubbed this "rice-water stool." Once this bowel movement began, odds were the victim would be dead in a matter of hours. After two days the pulse would be hardly detectable, and a mask of blue, leathery skin would have covered the face. As one doctor of the day described the final scene "countenance quite shrunk, eyes sunk, lips dark blue, as well as the skin of the lower extremities; the nails . . . . livid."[13]

Dr. Cantrell knew exactly what to do and put the *Dolphin* under quarantine immediately upon arrival. After the correct quarantine period, he boarded the ship and pronounced it free of disease. Dr. Cantrell not only served the town of Guysborough but the county as well, including Canso. In 1832 he became the Health Officer for all of Guysborough County as well as remaining a member of the Sydney Board of Health until 1835.

The only form of roads to most outports in those days were trails. It was on one of these that Dr. Cantrell was riding his horse on his way to New Harbour in August, 1838, when his horse got spooked and threw him. His body was found on the trail where a woodland brook crosses it. Cantrell's Lake,

---

[13] Steven Johnson, *The Ghost Map, The Story of London\s Most Terrifying Epidemic "*, Riverhead Books, New York, 2007, p. 35

Brook and Pond are landmarks today on the road which has replaced the trail. Dr. Cantrell was buried in Christ Church cemetery on September 2, 1838.

Dr. Edward Carritt   1800 - 1888

by Mark Haynes

Dr. Edward Carritt was born in Brigg, Lincolnshire, England on 26 July, 1800. In 1825 he attended the University of Edinburgh and graduated an LRCS (Licentiate of the Royal College of Surgeons) the following year. As soon as he received his degree in medicine, he married Miss Harriet Peacock, then a resident of Edinburgh, daughter of Robert Peacock of Solsgirth House, Perthshire. They immediately left for Nova Scotia, also in 1826. He initially set up his practise in Halifax where he is first mentioned in 1832 when he was assigned as a physician to the South Hospital, one of three cholera hospitals established in the city due to an outbreak of the disease in that year. Unfortunately the Colonial Council forgot to mention how he would be paid. This forced him to remind them in a letter dated September 5, that "until remuneration is agreed upon, I would not be accepting such an appointment".[14]

Also in 1832 he petitioned the House of Assembly to set up a Medical Department of the Poor to train doctors in the Halifax Poor House, thereby bringing free medical care to the poor and at the same time training doctors in Nova Scotia instead of in Britain. In his own words he points out:

> Such a school would release the public from the impositions and dangerous pretensions of emperies and persons deficient in medical education.[15]

---

[14] Allan Marble, *Physicians, Pestilence, and the Poor, a History of Medicine and Social Conditions in Nova Scotia 1800-1867,* Trafford, 2006, p. 157.

[15] Allan Marble, Ibid, p. 229

The Poor House was inspected for consideration of his suggestion and described at the time as housing 298 persons and found "every room from the Cellar to the Garret (attic) is filled to excess."[16] The building served as a General Hospital, a Lunatic Asylum, an Orphan House, a Sailor's Hospital and a Hospice. They noted that there was an absence of all comfort and all means of cleanliness and that provisions for bathing were non-existent because of the overcrowded state of the Asylum.[17] Despite the obvious need of a medical school and proper hospital, the support of the Grand Jury, the Commissioners of the Poor and the House of Assembly, Lieutenant Governor Maitland refused to back the scheme and the idea was abandoned.

Dr. Edward Carritt

In disgust Dr. Carritt moved to Truro in 1833 where he practised for a short time. While there he continued his efforts to instill professionalism in the medical community when in 1839 he established the Truro Literacy and Scientific Society. In the same year, Dr. Carritt, acting on a complaint of an improper amputation carried out by one Dr. Crowe, testified he also examined the amputation in question and concurred the patient's legs could not be saved. The patient in question was Abigail Alexander, a transient pauper, who spent several days in the woods when her legs became frozen. Thank heavens Dr. Carritt was quick at adopting new techniques and made sure chloroform anaesthesia, which had just been introduced into the colony, was used in the operation.

In 1842 Dr. Carritt moved permanently to Guysborough due to the picturesque seaside location of the town and the good health it provided.

---

[16] Allan Marble, Ibid, p. 230

[17] Allan Marble, Ibid, p. 231

Within a year of arrival he found the Guysborough Mechanics Institute on January 3, 1843 with himself as president and E. I. Cunningham as secretary. To his credit, the Institute acquired "an electrical machine and chemical apparatus"[18] for public demonstrations of how modern scientific machinery worked. Further testament of his professional nature comes in 1845 when he served as examiner for Henry Elliot of East River, St. Mary's, who was training to become a physician.[19]

His interests were not only with medicine but religion as well, doing guest sermons at Christ Church. In 1848 when an Anglican church was built in McNair's Cove, Dr. Carritt accompanied the Rev. C. J. Shreve at the opening ceremony.[20]

On February 4, 1850, he once again petitioned the House of Assembly for payment in a medical matter. The petition is worth quoting in full for it shows he did not reserve his services only to those who could afford them, but to any person in need, regardless of creed or social rank, worrying about remuneration later:

> A Petition of Edward Carritt of Guysborough, Surgeon, was presented
> by Mr. Marshall, and read, praying remuneration for Medical
> attendance upon, and Medicines furnished. Transient Paupers afflicted
> with Small Pox and for visiting, in his capacity as Health Officer, vessels
> arriving from Halifax after the breaking out of Small Pox there; and
> also for vaccinating a number of Indians and attending a sick Indian -
> all which services were performed by direction of the Board of Health.
> ORDERED, that so much of the Petition as related to services performed
> for the Indians, be referred to the Committee on Indian Affairs - and
> that remaining part thereof be referred to the Committee on Expenses

---

[18] John N. Grant, bio of *Samuel R. Russell, School Master, Inspector,* this publication.

[19] Allan Marble, Ibid, p. 96

[20] H. C. Hart, *History of the County of Guysborough,* Mika Publishing Co., Belleville, ON, 1975 p. 127

of sick Immigrants.[21]

For his services he was rewarded £22-4-0. Another interesting mention of Dr. Carritt is in 1854 when he submitted a Coroner's Report in the murder trial of the Snow brothers accused of killing two Casey children from Raspberry Cove. His investigation of the children's death states, "the boy died from drowning and the girl from injuries on Head and Body but by whom inflicted unknown".

When medicines claiming to be 'Indian' cures became all the rage in Nova Scotia, Dr. Carritt was quick to investigate and comment on their claims. They were being promoted by one Dr. Morris as a cure for smallpox. In a letter dated 6 May, 1861 to the Medical Society of Nova Scotia, Dr. Carritt commented on the unprofessional conduct of Dr. Morris in publishing his support of so called Indian remedies and recommended his license be suspended. Such was the influence Dr. Carritt had at this time on the medical community of the colony.

In 1866, when the Guysborough County Militia was formed, Dr. Carritt was made a 2nd Lieutenant in the unit.[22] His house in Guysborough still stands and is referred to as Carritt House to the present day, testament to his memory in the community. Sometimes one reads his last name with an 'e' on the end as in Carritte. His family added the 'e' to the end of the name to avoid pronouncing it like 'Carrot'.[23]

Dr. Carritt retired in 1884 due to ill health and the death of his beloved wife who passed away in that year at the age of 76. At the time of his retirement, he was the Dean of Serving Doctors in Nova Scotia. He moved to Dartmouth where he lived with his daughter, Mrs. Robert Cutler. Hilda Cox relates that the morning he left Guysborough, feeble and with assistance, he stopped at the top of McColl's Hill and "looked all around at the places he was

---

[21] Nova Scotia House of Assembly Journals, Vol. 20, Monday, 4th Feb., 1850.

[22] John A Morrison, *Down Guysborough Way,* unpublished manuscript, GHS, 1944, p. 121

[23] Ancestry.ca Message Board>surnames>Carritt, posted by Nancy Carritte, 22 Jan 2004.

leaving," and knew he would not be seeing it again.

He died Dartmouth in 1888 at the age of 88. His body was brought back to Guysborough and he was interred in Christ Church cemetery on October 31 of the same year. He was survived by three daughters, Eliza, Kate and Harriet, and two sons, Edward and William. A stained glass window in Christ the Good Shepherd chancel of Christ Church in Guysborough is in memory of this fine doctor. His family has since added the letter e to the end of their name so all descendants now spell their last name Carritte.

Louisa Sophia Clark 1814 – 1870

by: Chris Cook

One of the historic features of Christ Church Cemetery is the enduring presence of wrought-iron decorative fenced family burial plots. One such enclosure is that of Louisa Clark and her daughter Jane Richardson. Louisa Clark and her children came to Guysborough with her husband, William Clark, in 1850. They purchased a house and 55 acres on the peninsula where the current golf course operates, which they called *The Belmont*. Mrs. Hilda Cox, in her "As I Remember It discusses this family:

> *Still a third house stood on that slope in my young days, a way further*
> *to the east. When I first knew about it,...it was the home of the Clark*
> *family. Of Mr. Clark, I know almost nothing. The only record I can find*
> *of him is in a Belcher's Almanac of 1856 where his name (William*
> *Clark) is given as one of the Local Directors out of Halifax, for*
> *Guysborough, of the Nova Scotia Electric Telegraph Company, which*
> *had been incorporated by an Act of the Provincial Legislature in 1851.*
> *Mrs. Clark was a sister of Mrs. Judge Stewart Campbell (of*
> *Guysborough). She was a Richardson, a daughter of Matthew*
> *Richardson of Studley, Halifax, and had married another Richardson (I*
> *think a cousin) by whom she had several children. She was a widow,*
> *with Richardson children, when she married William Clark of Belmont,*
> *Halifax, and by him had two daughters, Laura and Ida. I do not know*
> *when or where, Mr. Clark died, but certainly he is not buried beside his*
> *wife in the old Anglican churchyard here. Her grave is enclosed by an*
> *iron fence, together with that of her daughter Jane Gordon, who "died*
> *at Belmont, universally loved, aged 22" (1864). The family called the*
> *property Belmont, perhaps because Mr. Clark had come from Belmont*
> *in, or perhaps near, Halifax. One of the Richardson children was a son*
> *"Banning" who became an Anglican clergyman and eventually a*
> *Venerable Archdeacon with a large church in London, Ontario. He told*
> *Abbie, whose mother Eva Campbell was his cousin, that as a boy he*

*helped his mother plant that row of trees which are still standing
though the old house has been gone for many years. He returned to
visit Guyborough several times during his lifetime. I remember his as a
very tall, dignified, white-haired old gentleman.*

Mrs. Cox continues, reflecting upon the location of the Belmont: ".. the names Cutler's Cove and Clark's Point are still used, often by a younger generation that has no idea of their origin. In my childhood day, Clark's Point was a favourite spot for Sunday school picnics, being accessible by boat as well as horse and buggy. The greater part of the Point was densely wooded with fir and spruce, but one large field, next to the harbour and enclosed by stone walls, was evidently reserved for hay. After the hay was cut, it was the perfect place for a picnic."

It is reported in the *Dictionary of Canadian Biography* that Louisa Clark was first married to James Richardson, an immigrant from Glasgow, Scotland. He moved to Halifax in 1802 and began a successful mercantile business. When he died in 1847, Louisa was left with six children to raise. Within three years, she had married William Clark, and removed to Guysborough. As the wife of the supervisor of the then wonderous telegraph service in the area, mother of an Anglican rector, and sister to Judge Campbell's wife, Louise was likely a very respected member of Guysborough Society during the mid-Victorian era.

Elias Cook Sr. 1721-1809

by Chris Cook

Thanks to the extensive research completed by the late Patricia Lumsden, we know that Elias Cook Sr. and his wife, Lydia immigrated to Halifax County from Marblehead, Massachusetts about 1761. There, he received a grant of 40 acres on Tangier Island to establish and settle a fishery. It is uncertain if this intended settlement ever came to fruition. Lumsden (2012) explains the likely motivation behind the move north by Elias and Lydia:

> Many of our Cook ancestors followed the sea. New England fisherman worked the Nova Scotian fishing grounds on a seasonal basis; catching, curing or drying their fish there, and returning with their goods ready for sale, to their New England homes for the winter months. By the terms of the Treaty of Paris (1763), U.S. fishermen were permitted to dry their catch on "any of the unsettled bays, harbors, and creeks of Nova Scotia, Magdalen Islands, and Labrador." No doubt Elias was familiar with the rich fishing grounds offered by the Chedabucto Bay area, which, in the early years, was as fine and as productive as any in the world. From the trade base at Canso, fresh and dried fish were shipped to New England and European ports.

In 1766, their son Benjamin was baptized at St. John's Anglican Church in Halifax, but by 1768 Elias and Lydia moved their family (which by this time had grown to 10 children) to the head of the Cove just south of Guysborough that would soon bare their name. Along with the families of Tobey, Peart, Horton, Hadley, Callahan, and Godfrey, the Cooks became lumped into a group to be known as the Pre-loyalists. For the next 15-20 years, they were the only known English settlers on this coast. It wasn't until the influx of the Loyalists in Guysborough, in 1784 that Elias and his family actually owned the land on which they were living. It is reported in an appeal made by the Crown's surveyor, Charles Morris, that despite the Cook's Cove area being granted to the members of the 60th Regiment, the Cooks and other families should be given the land first as "they had built houses and made considerable improvement on the same" and it had been settled by them since 1768. The Crown approved and by 1787, the Cooks finally owned the property on which they had been living for two decades. With property ownership comes taxation. The first assessment was conducted in 1791. In 1793, there were six adult Cook men listed as heads of households in the Cooks Cove area: Elias Sr. and sons Elias Jr., James, John (Jack), Benjamin, and also Elias Cook III.

Gravestones of (left to right); Elias Cook Sr. 1809, Philomela Cook 1809 and Benjamin Cook 1833.

Elias Cook Sr. died in 1809 at the age of 88. It is unknown where Lydia, Elias' wife, is buried, and she may have predeceased the opening of the cemetery in 1786, and therefore is laid to rest at some unknown location on the family farm. The family cannot trace Elias' lineage past his grandfather, Elias Cook. He was married in Marblehead Mass in 1698, but nothing prior is known of the family.

There are four sons of Elias' and Lydia's known to be buried at Christ Church. Elias (1797), Benjamin (1833), John (Jack) (1840, and Edward (1846). Elias Cook Jr., farmed and fished at Cook's Cove. In 1769 he married Anna Cleaves of Beverly Mass, daughter of Ambrose Cleaves, a partner in the Land Bank of Beverly of 1740. They had 11 children. Elias Jr.., did not appear to have moved from the New England coast with his parents and siblings in the 1760's until they received a grant of land in the late 1780's. All 11 of their children were born and baptized in Beverly, Mass. Elias Jr. died quite young in 1797. In the records of Christ Church the cause of death was *of the gravel*. This was the term given to kidney stones. This is a male hereditary condition in the Cook family; and has found its way to the present day generation of the family. Anna Cook was also buried at Christ Church on January 23, 1812 at the age of 69. Their son Winthrop Cook (Cooke) moved to the Isaac's Harbour area of Guysborough County, and all Cook(e) descendants in the communities of Isaac's Harbour, Goldboro, Stormont, and Country Harbour can trace their lineage to Winthrop.

Very little is known about Edward Cook; other than he was born in 1752 and lived to be 94 years of age; being buried at Christ Church cemetery August, 1846. Family records only know his wife to be Elizabeth, and they had the one daughter Elizabeth who was born in 1812, when Edward was 60 years old. Elizabeth Cook (mother) was buried at Christ Church in 1843 at the age of 61.

Benjamin Cook was born in 1766 and died in 1833. His first wife was Philomela Hull. They had at least six children. She died in 1809 at age 40 during childbirth, according to the church records. The baby also did not survive. She and Benjamin are buried beside his father Elias at Christ Church cemetery. Benjamin married a second time In 1810, Lucy Cameron. He and Lucy had 8 children. At least two children were born when Benjamin was in his 60's. Benjamin and his families lived in Cook's Cove, on the "family farm" ownership followed his line of descendants. After Benjamin's death, Lucy remarried, and several of the younger children relocated moved to Queen's County, N.S.

Today, no Cook children remain in the cove so named after this family. A far cry from the school records of the mid 1820's, which lists 60% of the entire school attendance of 45 students, as Cooks.

John "Jack" Cook   1752 – 1840

By: Chris Cook

From the sources available, the life of John "Jack" Cook, could easily play out in the Hollywood genre of an 18th century frontiersman; doing what was necessary, and clever, to survive on the north-eastern coast of Nova Scotia. His life was long, colourful, and adventurous. For at least three generations before Jack Cook would set foot in Cook's Cove (approximately 2 km south east of Guysborough), his father, grandfather and great-grandfather, each named Elias, would work in the fishery. The family moved between Marblehead, Gloucester, and Beverly Massachusetts. In the 1768, when Jack was approximately 16, the family eventually decided to settle in one place. With the availability of land and excellent fishing in eastern Nova Scotia, Elias Cook decided to clear the hillside at the head of Cook's Cove and "put down roots."

The Cooks appear to have been settled at Cook's Cove for approximately 20 years before receiving an official grant for their land. Jack Cook received 300 acres and his father, Elias, 200. Part of the original grant remains in the family today.

From the records that are available, it appears that Jack was in his 30's before marrying. Jack appears to have lived the life of the wild rover over the previous decade. A.C. Jost discusses the escapades of young Jack in the early 1780's:

> *The story involves a love match frowned upon by unrelenting parents, a running away from home as a member of one of the fishing crews engaged in fishing off the Canso Banks, a ship wreck and salvation by the Indians and the enforced presence of the rescued in an Indian wigwam during the winter months, of sickness among the Indians, and their gratitude for the assistance which they received from the visitor, of return home to find that objections to the union had been withdrawn, the marriage and the return to the scene of the winter's sojourn.*

Concerning the "love match frowned upon," Jack Cook married

Elizabeth Tobey, whose father Nathanial, received a grant of land directly *across* the small waters of Cook's Cove from the Cook grant. Elizabeth Tobey could trace her lineage directly to Stephan Hopkins of the Mayflower; as her mother was formerly Elizabeth Hopkins. Did the Cook's and Tobey's engage in some sort of local squabble over property or fishing rights, or did the dislike between the two families go back generations to the "New England coast?" The reasons behind the frowned upon union can only be speculative.

Jack and Elizabeth would have at least six children between 1786 and 1798. Their children and grandchildren mostly dispersed from the local area; settling in River Bourgeoise and Arichat Cape Breton, as well as the south shore of Nova Scotia. After having lived a winter with the local Aboriginal people, Jack and his family appear to have established a close alliance with them; and likely co-habitated peacefully and respectfully. Mrs. H.C. Hart relays the following in her *History of the County of Guysborough:*

> *From frequent kindly intercourse with the Indians Messers Cook had made themselves familiar with the Micmac language and customs and had become their firm allies. A vessel belong to Chedabucto was chased up the bay by a privateer and when near the harbour Mr. Cook, who was watching his neighbours distressed condition, ran quickly from his house shouting some peculiar cry previously agreed upon in case of trouble, when so many Indians came rushing and whooping to their canoes upon the shore that the privateer turned and fled in dismay.*

Mrs. H. C. Hart also relates a significantly dangerous event in Jack's life; which found Jack kidnapped by unfriendly privateers. She describes:

> *One day, while Mr. Jack Cook was out fishing, he was captured by the noted Paul Jones. The pirate compelled Mr. Cook to pilot him around the coast, and show him the way into certain harbours, using thumbscrews and other persuasive powers to affect his object. He was thus unwillingly employed for three weeks, and then set on shore. Some of his adventures came to the ears of a captain of a cutter upon the coast, and the poor man was seized and tried as an accomplice of the celebrated sea rover. His innocence was easily proved, however, by*

the unanimous testimony of his neighbours.

Before Jack was 40, his life was filled with ample adventure and potentially fatal situations for a dozen men. As time passed, Jack took up entrepreneurship. He was known to be a shopkeeper, and kept a store in the village of Guysborough. He was appointed "Culler and Surveyor of Fish" in 1785. He brought legal action against persons caught stealing from his store to the Court of General Sessions of the Peace on several occasions. In 1791, two cases were heard for persons stealing potatoes and moose meat. Each party was found guilty and received 39 stripes on the "naked back at the Public Whipping Post." They were also ordered to repay John for his losses. (Lumsden, 2012). After these events, there are no other documents concerning Jack until his burial in Christ Church cemetery in February of 1840 at the age of 88.

Jack's father, Elias Sr. (1809), and brothers: Elias (1797), Benjamin (1833), and Edward (1846), are also buried in Christ Church cemetery.

Elizbeth Goldsbury Cutler 1766 - 1832

by Jamie Grant

Surprisingly little is known about the lives of our pioneer women other than that they lived lives of uncertainty, toil and hardship. The historical record is so male oriented that it renders women virtually invisible. Even the baptismal records which name the child, the father and without fail the clergyman, often refers to the mother only as 'Mrs' or 'and wife of'. Elizabeth Cutler's life is a refreshing exception to the rule.

Her birth in 1766 to the prosperous Massachusetts farmer Samuel and Rhoda (Partridge) Goldsbury coincided with the rising tensions which would soon erupt as civil war in the American colonies. Little 'Betsy' Goldsbury must have experienced the terror common to children in strife torn areas. Her home was repeatedly attacked and her father beaten to the point of death by mobs because of his openly Loyalist stance. When the shooting began, Samuel left the family to join the fight believing that in his absence they would be left alone. In this lie was mistaken. Forced from their home by continual harassment, they were harried from place to place for years before reuniting with Samuel briefly in Rhode Island. After a short sojourn there, they were able to reach safety in British held, but war torn New York City. Here in 1783 she met and married Lt. Thomas Cutler. She was seventeen and he was thirty-one.

Shortly after their marriage, they departed for 'the wilderness of Nova Scotia', landing at the ill fated settlement at Port Mouton. Here they survived a winter of privation and a devastating spring fire which resulted in the abandonment of the site. By mid June, 1784, at eighteen years of age and six months pregnant, she was off the mouth of Guysborough Harbour on another transport ship. As Lt. William Campbell was preparing to go ashore to procure a pilot to show them the way into the harbour, Betsy playfully warned him 'not to lose his heart' to the girl they could see tending the fish flakes on Long Beach. He did 'lose his heart' and thus the future Sir William and Lady Hannah Campbell met. Despite the tribulations of her childhood, she had emerged cheerful, positive and resilient, traits which would serve her well as a pioneer woman.

There is another well remembered antidote that reveals her resourcefulness while still a teenager. Hilda Cox tells the story as she heard it a century after its occurrence:

> One day when her husband was away and no men were within call, she saw some Indians approaching. Though they may have been on a friendly errand, she took no chances. She was making bread at the time, and quickly touched the face of her sleeping baby with dabs of dough, adding touches of molasses. And when the Indians came to the door, she pointed to the baby and said simply, 'small pox' and at that dreaded word, the Indians fled.[24]

If H.C. Hart's account of a contemporary raid on William Nixon's store by the Mik'maq at the same time is accurate (see biography of William Nixon), Mrs. Cutler's actions deserve another level of admiration.[25]

Her early years here must have been demanding despite the fact her husband's 'half pay' status as an officer ensured advantages unknown to most. However, anything even approaching ease was still in the distant future.

Elizabeth Cutler raised a family of five, all of whom enjoyed more than average success while she attended to the duties incumbent on the wife of the county's leading man. She also found time to act as secretary treasurer and depositary of the Ladies' Benevolent Society which met at her home monthly to make clothing for the poor. She filled this role until failing health forced her to resign. Her life ended three years later in 1832.

One hopes she found comfort having four of her children (one son and three daughters) and many grandchildren living within a mile of the log house she and Thomas continued to occupy until the end or their lives. Together they accumulated considerable wealth and many possessions, some of which Thomas states in his will he had distributed among their daughters "as directed by Betsy" a few days before she died.

With a May/October wedding it's normal to wonder about the

---

[24] Hilda Cox, *As I Remember It..*

[25] H.C Hart, *History of the County of Guysboroough,* *P. 51*

motivation for the union. Thomas's actions attest to his devotion to her, from the naming of his first ship *The Betsy,* to his appointing her executrix of his will and in its preamble stating her efforts were as much responsible for his 'material advance' as his own. Though we have less evidence of her feelings, being loved, valued and respected tends to warm the heart. One hopes that after such a trying life he brought her joy.

Robert Molleson Cutler   1784 - 1883

by Mark Haynes

For much of his adult life Robert Cutler was the most influential man in Guysborough County. His Loyalist parents, Thomas and Elizabeth (Goldsbury) Cutler, arrived in Guysborough in mid June 1784, four months before his birth on October 9th of this year. His father Thomas had spent the dying months of the American Revolutionary War as assistant barracks master at the British Army's headquarters in New York. Through this position he got to know Wagon Master General Robert Molleson for whom he named his only son. On arrival in Guysborough, Thomas Cutler opened a store at Cutler's Cove (named after him) and became a prominent merchant. Due to his legal training, he also became a justice of the peace as well as the first town clerk.

So Robert, like many boy wonders before and since, enjoyed a head start in life. In 1790 at the age of six, he was granted a town lot in Guysborough. Then in 1793, when he was nine years old, he received another 280 acre land grant. Ironically this was almost three times the amount of land allotted to disbanded soldiers who had actually fought for as long as eight years for their country. Though there was a school in town by 1790, it seems the Cutler children (Robert had four younger sisters), were taught privately at home. Robert's education was augmented by his early entry into his father's business which was multi faceted - a general store, a real estate and mortgage office, shipping and much more. He learned the rudiments of law, accounting, customs regulations, banking and insights into the workings of government when his father became an MLA .

One of the more interesting stories told of young Robert was when he was a baby. His mother, alarmed one day to see approaching canoes filled with Indians, realized their intentions weren't friendly. She ran to the cradle where Robert lay, picked him up, daubed his face with molasses and flower, then held him up at the door and called "Smallpox". That was a dreaded word to the Indians as well as the Whites. The Indians withdrew leaving the Cutlers alone.

In 1808 Robert was named Lieutenant-Colonel of the 19th Battalion of

the Sydney County Militia . The
following year on Dec. 2, 1809 at
the age of 25, he married Sophia
Reynolds, the daughter of a
prominent Halifax business man. As
the years passed he accumulated
many more positions such as
postmaster, clerk of the Crown,
Custos Rotolorum (Warden),
president of the local Farmer's
Society and from 1818 to 1820 he
was an MLA. On April 13, 1834,
Robert Cutler was appointed as a
Member of the Legislative Council,
a body like a provincial senate, the
"upper house", as a supporter of
the Conservative Party. This
Legislative body came about as an
appeasement to the reform
movement which had been
simmering in the colony for some
time.

The Hon. R. M. Cutler

Robert took over his father's store at the head of Cutler's Cove as well
as opened another one at the Guysborough Intervale where the Cross Roads
are. Like his father, Robert took an active role in the Anglican faith and paid for
a pulpit, reading desk and altar for Christ Church. On learning the congregation
at the Intervale could not be accompanied comfortably in a private home, in
1835 he placed at their disposal the store he owned there. He then installed a
pulpit and stove so they could enjoy their services in all seasons. The foundation
of this store is still visible today adjacent to the Guysborough Antigonish Rd.
near the crossroads. His store remained the sole place of worship until a proper
Anglican church was built at the Intervale in 1850.

Among his many achievements was the establishment of a packet
service between Guysborough and Arichat, then the commercial centre of Cape
Breton. The first boat he used on this run was the sloop *Kingbird*. The historian

Harriet Hart recounts how Robert came about acquiring it. The ship was seized for smuggling by the authorities near Canso. Due to it being built in the United States, it could not be registered in the U.K. or any of its colonies and consequently could not continue to be used as a packet. As a result it went up for sale and Robert bought it. In addition he financed the construction of the ships *Billow* (1822), *Guysborough* (1827) and *Margaret* (1829) adding to his fleet. Being concerned about the safety of his ships, he and seventy-two others petitioned the colonial government in 1842 for a "Beacon Light" at the mouth of Guysborough Harbour. The Legislative Assembly responded by building a lighthouse there the following year.

Robert Cutler's dominance of local affairs was so complete that the *Reformer Press* used his *Cutler's Compact* as an example of nepotism in the extreme. It was claimed that fifty-seven government appointments had been awarded to nineteen "compact" members. The influence of Robert Cutler was emphasized when he and MLA John Marshall accompanied the Governor of the colony of Nova Scotia, Sir James Kempt, from Guysborough to Antigonish during his first and only visit to the area in 1822.His influence didn't end at the county or provincial capitals either. For example, he was on intimate terms with Sir William Campbell, the Chief Justice of Upper Canada who his father trained in law.

The Hon. R.M. Cutler died on May 2, 1883 at the age of ninety-eight (rounded up to 99 on his gravestone), at his home at Guysborough and was interred in Christ Church cemetery. He was predeceased by his wife Sophia who died in 1849 and survived by his children including Caroline (1832) who married Father of Confederation Willam Le Vesconte, Elizabeth (1810) who married High Sheriff Murdock MacLean, Sophia (1812) who married High Sheriff James Marshall and Harriet (1814), Thomas (1816), Robert (1819), William (1822) and lastly Frances (1828).

The gravestone of R.M. Cutler

Thomas Cutler   1752 - 1837

from The Dictionary of Canadian Biography, Vol. VII, 1836-1850.

by Judith Tulloch

CUTLER, THOMAS, lawyer, jp, office holder, judge, militia officer, politician, and merchant; b. 11 Nov. 1752 in Boston, fifth child of Thomas Cutler and Sarah Reade; m. 3 March 1783 Elizabeth Goldsbury, probably in New York City, and they had five children; d. 8 Feb. 1837 in Guysborough, N.S.

Thomas Cutler was descended from a family resident in Massachusetts for more than a century. Educated at Yale College, he graduated in 1771 and settled at Hatfield, Mass., where he is said to have studied law. He joined the British forces in Boston at the outbreak of the American revolution and in September 1778 was proscribed in the Massachusetts Banishment Act. Serving first as a captain in the Volunteers of New England, by the end of the war he was established in New York as an assistant barrack master. In September 1783 he was commissioned ensign in the Orange Rangers, apparently because regimental rank offered greater possibilities for compensation and advancement.

Cutler and his wife were evacuated to Nova Scotia late in 1783 as part of the refugee group known as the Associated Departments of the Army and Navy, composed principally of headquarters staff. The group first settled at Port Mouton on the South Shore, but after a harsh winter marked by quarrels with other loyalists moved east to Chedabucto Bay. On 21 June 1784 they landed at the head of the bay, where the village of Guysborough was already beginning to take shape. Along with his fellow veterans, Cutler was granted farm land along the Milford Haven (Guysborough) River as well as town and water lots in the village.

Thomas Cutler's house at Cutler's Cove, Guysborough. His house
is visible to the extreme left. Hilda Cox described it in her memoir,
As I Remember It, "The old Cutler house was still standing when I
was young. This was in the field at the head of what we call Cutler's
Cove. The house itself stood well up on the brow of the hill facing
the cove. It was long and low and had been made of logs. We could
not see the logs themselves as they had been boarded over."

Cutler's legal training and administrative experience stood him in good
stead in his new home. He sat as one of the justices of the peace at the first
sessions for the district, held in November 1785, and served as the first town
clerk for Guysborough. He was later appointed judge of probate for Sydney
County and a justice of the Inferior Court of Common Pleas. For many years
Cutler held a special licence to conduct marriages. He was commissioned
lieutenant-colonel of the newly organized Sydney County militia in July 1794.

In 1793 Cutler was elected to the House of Assembly for Sydney
County. He and fellow refugee John Stuart were the first local residents to
represent the district, which had returned two Haligonians in the previous
election. Cutler took little part in the work of the assembly: he attended only
two sessions and did not contest the election of 1799.

Like most pioneer inhabitants of rural Nova Scotia, Cutler turned his
hand to a variety of occupations. He continued his legal practice and is said to

have trained William Campbell*, later chief justice of Upper Canada. Cutler is chiefly remembered, however, for his commercial activities. As early as 1792 he was listed as a merchant in the district assessment rolls, and in the 1790s he was appointed to several local customs offices usually held by prominent traders. Cutler also took an interest in the agricultural development of the district, serving as one of the first vice-presidents of the Guysborough and Manchester Farmer Society, organized in 1819 in response to the enthusiasm generated throughout the province by John Young's Agricola letters.

Thomas Cutler's table monument in Christ Church Cemetery.

Local tradition honoured Cutler as "King" Cutler, reflecting his widespread influence in the county. Eulogized for his "strict and known integrity, loyalty, and ability," he is remembered as one of the founders of Guysborough.

Sources:
PANS, MG 100, 129, no.40; RG 1, 169, 171–73, 223. Novascotian, or Colonial Herald, 23 Feb. 1837. F. B. Dexter, Biographical sketches of the graduates of Yale College, with annals of the college history (6v., New York and New Haven,

Conn., 1885–1912), 3. J. H. Stark, *The Loyalists of Massachusetts and the other side of the American Revolution* (Boston, [1907]). Harriet Cunningham Hart, *History of the county of Guysborough* (Belleville, Ont., 1975). A. C. Jost, *Guysborough Sketches and other Essays* (Guysborough, N.S., 1950). Hilda Cox, *As I Remember It*, GHS, 2018

John Davis ? – 1804

by: Jamie Grant

John Davis, like most buried in Christ Church Cemetery, was of the "common folk" of whom Abraham Lincoln said "God must have loved best since He made so many of them." Davis arrived in Guysborough with the Associated Departments of the Army and Navy, June 1784; accompanied by his wife Mary and their three children: Rebecca, John and Catherine, each under the age of 10. Two more were born after their arrival, William and Elizabeth Mary. His land grant of 300 acres, one hundred for himself and the other 200 because of his four dependants, suggests he was either a disbanded Private or had filled a minor role in the Civil Department. This is about all we would know about John Davis, if not for a singular event which reveals something of his character and sheds some light on the community and the tenor of the times.

The follow extract from the Court of Sessions, County of Sydney (Guysborough), February 10, 1795, tells this story:

> *John Davis of Guysborough, Yeoman – Complained to the Court – That he had formerly bound his daughter, Rebecca Davis, a minor, unto the Rev. Mr. Peter Delaroche – and that the same Mr. Delaroche had (in his life time) assigned his said daughter, unto Dr. Dennis Heffernan – to give him the remainder of her time – The Court having taken into consideration the said Complaint – and the parties – having been present – and heard – they do consider, that the said Transfer of Assignment of the said Apprentice to said Dr. Heffernan to be illegal – therefore the said Dr. Heffernan has no Claim upon the said Apprenticeship.*

It is clear that Davis, a self-employed farmer, would not suffer injustice without a fight belying the American stereotype of the Loyalists as craven toadies. In a society as divided by class as by race or religion, he sought justice from three Judges (ex-military officers on half pay) against Dr. Heffernan, Naval Surgeon, one of their own. As well, the Justices, as they were known, would have been most aware that finding in favour of Davis would sully the name of the beloved Rev. Delaroche, then dead only three weeks. That they did so reflects well on both their understanding of the law and their principles. Their decision also reflects the often noted sense of equality that seemed to prevail as an earmark of the community.

It might be explained that the apprenticing of a minor, was a common practice at the time. Rev. Delaroche had bound his ten year old son Alexander, to John Britt, a carpenter of Crow Harbour (Queensport) three years earlier in 1792. Apprenticeship agreements were formal legal agreements, carefully worded to outline the duties, obligations and privileges of both parties. The "master" agreed to teach a skill, while the apprentice supplied labour to pay for his/her keep and trade training. Apprenticeship periods varied, but were usually for seven years, and the agreement, once signed, could not be altered without the approval of both parties. This was the point of Davis' successful suit. Was John Davis a 18th Century Viola Desmond? Perhaps, but either way, he made his point.

Edmund DeFrancheville 1810 – 1876

by Jamie Grant

One of the more distinctive gravestones in Christ Church Cemetery is the tall, red-granite obelisk erected in the memory of Edmund DeFrancheville. Harriet Hart, author of the *History of the County of Guysborough*, who knew him well, summarized his life as follows:

> *Edmund H. Francheville was the eldest son of J. G. Francheville Esq., of Halifax, and grandson of Dr. Francheville of H.M. Ship Wardner. He was born April 7, 1810, at Alexandria, Virginia, whither his father had removed and married, and where he died when his son was only five years old. When he was seven years of age, his mother was prevailed upon to allow him to remove to Guysboro, to reside with his aunt, Mrs. Ann Mueller (Miller). Here he grew up, was educated, and continued to reside. He became High Sheriff on the death of Murdoch McLean Esq. He was Lloyd's Agent and United States Vice Consul. His commission as Magistrate dated from 1842."*

It might be emphasized that these positions made him one of the principal men of affairs in the County, and that it was while he was in office, that Guysborough enjoyed its era of greatest prosperity during the "Golden Age of Sail." Under the Reciprocity Treaty with the United States, hundreds of American fishing vessels plied local waters resulting in many conflicts with merchants, inshore fishermen, government officials and others, which as U.S. Vice Consul, DeFrancheville would have been expect to resolve. As Lloyd's Agent, every ships' launch, wreck or mishap in the area would have required his attention and the position of High Sheriff was both complex and challenging, demanding his presence in all parts of the County. He was also active in Church and community being among other things a leader of the Temperance movement.

His 1843 marriage to Sarah Peart produced seven children, only one of whom, Charles (mariner, merchant, MLA and MLC), passed the name to descendants, some of whom still reside in Guysborough. Unfortunately, several children died well before maturity. George died at age 4 in 1861, and two other of their sons, Alfred (17) and Joseph (16) died in 1867; six months apart. Their daughters Eugenia and Sadie died in 1886 and 1888 at ages 25 and 35 respectively. They are all interred at Christ Church. Edmund DeFrancheville died in 1876 at the age of 66, his many exertions perhaps, shortening his life. His wife, Sarah passed in 1903 at the age of 84.

One colourful story remains in local tradition of the specific duties required of Sheriff Edmund DeFrancheville. It was claimed by the late Mrs. Mabel Hemming that her grandfather (Sheriff Edmund DeFrancheville), was required to read the Riot Act at a local Tavern to quell a civil disturbance which he felt endangered the public peace.

48

Rev. Peter De La Roche 1732 -1795

From: Harriet Cunningham Hart's *History of the County of Guysborough*

Unless Nicholas Denys or any other of the Huguenot Proprietors of Chedabuctou had chaplains in connection with their settlements, the Rev. Peter de La Roche was the first Protestant clergyman in this part of the country. He was a native of Geneva, Switzerland, sent to Nova Scotia by the Society for the Propagation of the Gospel, and was ordained to the care of Lunenburg in 1771. His native language was French, and he had acquired fluency in English. Now, many of his parishioners being German, he took up this study in his scant leisure, and was soon able to officiate in three languages. He wrote a commentary on the four Gospels, published several sermons at his own expense to be given away, and sent others to be printed in the *Halifax Gazette*. His salary was very small and he suffered many privations during the American war.

He came to Chedabucto in 1786; his note in the parish records says, "on private business," but his ministry to the people at that time resulted in an application being made to the Society for the Propagation of the Gospel "from the new setters at Manchester, in the County of Sydney, where they have been for two years without any clergyman, begging that they will take their distressed case under consideration and send them a missionary." they asked for Mr. De La Roche as he had officiated among them much to their satisfaction for a month last summer, and baptized 144 of their children. They offered to defray his expenses in moving, to provide him a house and find him fuel. The Society decided to grant their application and directed Mr. De La Roche to remove thither. The mandate for his induction addressed to Nathan Hubbill and James Wyatt, was issued by Governor Parr, June 14, 1787.

He arrived at Manchester (as it was then called) with his family July 6, 1787, and lived first in a house belonging to Benjamin Elliot, until the rectory was built on the corner of Prince and Main Streets nearly opposite the present Post Office. On August 6th, a meeting was called when the first church officers were appointed. These were Nathan Hubbill and James Wyatt, church wardens; the vestrymen being Thomas Cunningham, William Brown Hulme, John Grant, John

Nash, John Ingersoll and George Strahan. The clerk of the vestry was Augustus Fricke.

Gravestones of Peter and Ann De La Roche in Christ Church cemetery.

Mr. De La Roche reports to the Society in England, October 11, 1788, "The number of heads of families is supposed to be in Guysborough - 225, in Manchester - 99, so that upon a moderate computation there are about 1,200 souls. This mission is 55 leagues from Halifax. " He had baptized 42 children, 2 adults and married 12 couples.

In 1792 Mr. De La Roche speaks of the healthfulness of the climate in which he is of opinion, "none can exceed it, or avail more to the restoring of persons under lingering disorders." That in the five years he had been there he had buried only 39, of which number 16 were under twelve years of age, whereas in the same space of time he had baptized 229 besides adults.

In another letter written in 1792, he writes that his parish, being so large and the distance from the church to some of the inhabitants very great, he had encouraged three of the districts to meet together at one of their houses, to have prayers and a sermon read, for which purpose he had lent them the homilies and Tillotson's sermons. He spends one Sunday in a year with them which is all that he can do considering the distance and the difficulties in going thither which can only be by sea (probably Country Harbour).

A Chapel of Ease had lately been opened by the people in one district called Union Chapel, from the circumstance of their having, though of different denominations, agreed to join in one congregation. He requested some prayer books, which were sent to him from England. The Society for the Propagation of the Gospel paid Mr. De La Roche a stipend of 50-0-0 pounds sterling per annum. From the people he received very little. The Society also paid 10-0-0 pounds sterling per annum towards the support of school masters, who taught under the supervision of the clergy, and acted in some measure as catechists. Patrick Patton was the school master in Guysborough from about 1790 to 1818. He had been a sergeant in the 71st Regiment. Matthew Gregg, who had served as quartermaster in the South Carolina Royalists, was school master at Stormont. John Campbell, Sergeant in the King's Carolina Rangers, taught at Stormont, at Boylston and at County Harbour in all about 40 years. The Rev. Peter de La Roche passed away from earth on January 20, 1795. The many hardships he had endured as a good soldier of Christ, sapped the foundations of his strength, and he ceased from his labours at the comparatively early age of 63 years.

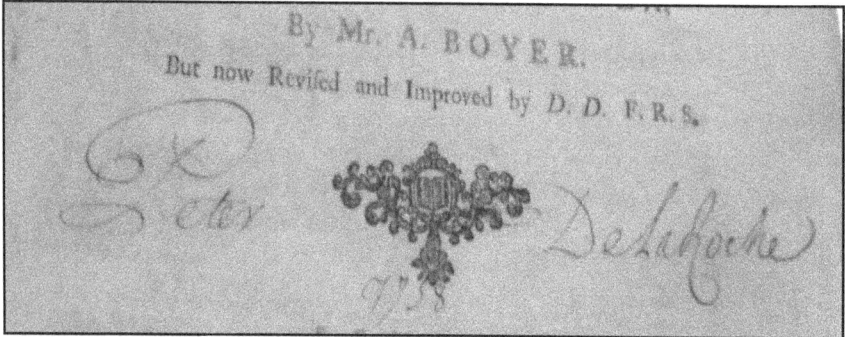

Signature of Peter De La Roche from his personal dictionary.

Dinah 1721 - 1807

by Mark Haynes

Listed in Christ Church burial records is the name Dinah. In all likelihood she is the mother of Hannah Lining. According to historian Ruth Whitehead, "Since Dinah was born around 1721 and Hannah about 1749, it is almost certain they were mother and daughter. Their ancestors had probably been slaves on this same property as there are Dinahs and Hannahs recorded in the death inventories of the family (Lining and Hill), of their enslaver for generations."[1]

Born a slave on the plantation of Dr. John Lining in South Carolina, her routes to the plantation go deep unlike more recent acquisitions. According to the "Account Book of Austin and Laurens, 1751", Dr. Lining was busy purchasing slaves:

1 July 1751
Doct. John Linning, 2 Men payub, per Bond this date on 1ˢᵗ November next with Ints. [interest][2]

In 1780 she and her daughter escaped. The opportunity arose when British forces under General Sir Henry Clinton landed just south of Charlestown and occupied the Lining plantation known as Hillsborough. He made the plantation his temporary military headquarters. Prior to this Dinah's daughter Hannah had been injured in one eye and consequently was partially blind. Due to this injury she was not accepted into the Wagon Master or Royal Artillery Departments. This meant neither she nor her mother, who was too old for

---

[1] Ruth Holmes Whitehead, *Black Loyalists, Southern Settlers of Nova Scotia's First Free Black Communities*, Nimbus Publishing, P. 178.

[2] Ibid, p. 19/20

heavy work, could earn their freedom. None-the-less for some reason General Clinton admired the two of them and certified them free. He issued them a pass allowing them to travel to New York as long as they stayed within the British lines. Getting there was their responsibility.

Somehow they made it to New York where they stayed until passage to Nova Scotia eventually availed itself. In 1783 they boarded the Brig *Elijah* to Port Mouton and then onward to Chedabucto (Guysborough) in 1784. While registering their names in the *Book of Negroes* before getting on the ship, Hannah took on the last name of Lining, the name of her slave owner. Dinah did not. She simply refused to adopt the name of a slave owner as her own. She is listed in the *Book of Negroes* as, "Dianah, 62, ordinary wench. Formerly resided in Charlestown, SC. Left enslaver John Lynning [Dr. John Lining] of Charlestown, SC in 1780. Certified free as per General Musgrave Cerificate."

Sometime during this period at the age of 38, probably aboard ship, Hannah met and married James Lenox. Dinah and Hannah were baptized at Christ Church on July 30, 1787. In the same year both Hannah and her husband received a grant of land at Tracadie but didn't move there. This was probably due to her husband's state of health for he died soon after in 1788 at the age of 24. He was interred in Christ Church Cemetery.

According to Ruth Whitehead, Hannah married again and spent the rest of her life in the village of Guysborough working and taking care of her mother. She must have taken good care of her for she lived to the ripe old age of 85, a very old age for this time. Dinah died in 1807. No headstone was erected to mark the place of internment in Christ Church Cemetery. Her grave was marked by what was described as ancient ornamental trees and summer flowers.[3] There are no surviving records indicating what the name of Hannah's second husband was. Though she was also buried in the cemetery, the last name she was buried under is not known.

---

[3]Records of Christ Church Anglican, Guysborough, MFN #11,390, NSA

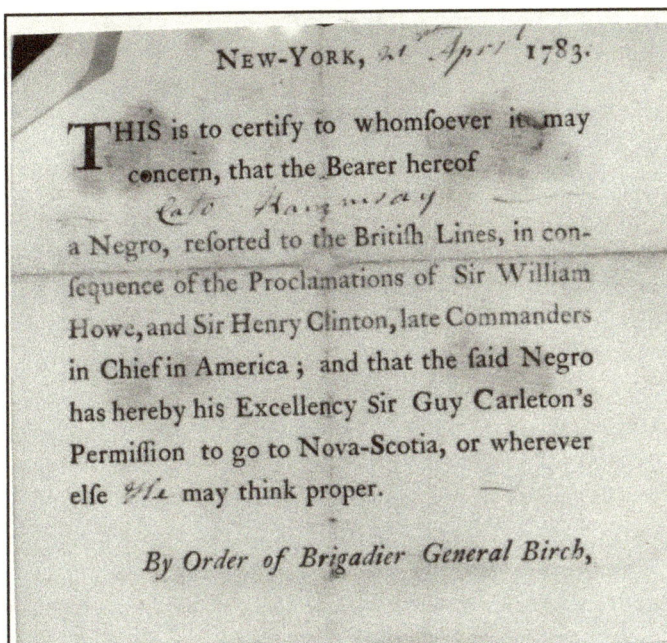

NEW-YORK, 21 April 1783.

THIS is to certify to whomfoever it may concern, that the Bearer hereof

Cato Ramsay

a Negro, reforted to the Britifh Lines, in confequence of the Proclamations of Sir William Howe, and Sir Henry Clinton, late Commanders in Chief in America; and that the faid Negro has hereby his Excellency Sir Guy Carleton's Permiffion to go to Nova-Scotia, or wherever elfe *He* may think proper. —

By Order of Brigadier General Birch,

Example of the kind of pass Hannah and her mother Dinah received to travel through British controlled territory. Guysborough is named after Sir Guy Carleton while two black communities in Nova Scotia were named Birchtown in honour of Brigadier General Birch. (Ruth Holmes Whitehead, *Black Loyalists,* Nimbus Pub., 2011)

William Foster 1748 – 1833

by Chris Cook

William Foster was one of the many members of the "The Associated Departments of the Army and Navy" who received land grants and a Town Lot in Guysborough in 1784. A.C. Jost describes this hodge-podge of desperate refugees as such:

> Many of the persons making up this group were among the last to leave New York. There were many in it who had not been members of line Regiments. Some had been named in the Massachuset Banishment Act. The 71st and 22nd Regiment were represented, although how many there were from each unit is now difficult to say. Nor can it be told how many had been in distinctively Loyalist units, such as the Tarleton or British Legion. The name implied, too, that naval personnel were included, as well as members of the land forces and the staffs, so that it was a heterogeneous grouping of persons who had little but their need in common. (Jost, 150 p. 297).

William received the town lot of L 12 in the Northeast Division of Guysborough, and 62.5 acres of "front lands" and 187.5 acres of "back lands." The distance from the village to the "front lands" was often lengthy, which caused a large number of the early settlers to sell their town lots and carve out a homestead on their front lands instead. Foster did the opposite and remained in the village.

He persevered through the early difficult years of the settlement, and by 1791 married Mary (Margaret) Cook (1772-1825), grand-daughter of the first Cook settler, Elias, of nearby Cook's Cove. Between 1792 and 1810, they had nine children, and it is known that three of their sons: James (1807-1833), John (1794-1845), and Thomas (1808-1873), and two of their grandchildren (Anna and Elias) are also buried at Christ Church cemetery. There were likely other members of the family whose burials at Christ Church were unrecorded during the time of Rev. Weeks. The grandchildren of William Foster, listed above, were the children of Elias and Elizabeth Foster. Their house and his carpentry business were directly across Pleasant Street from the cemetery; however neither are listed in the burial records. The Anglican records do state that William Foster "died very suddenly" at the age of 85.

At least three generations of the Foster family lived within the shadow of Christ Church along Pleasant street. William Foster established himself as an tavern-keeper. He was granted a "free-license" for "the sale of intoxicating liquors" in 1802. Foster's Inn was located on the corner of Pleasant and Church Street, kitty-corner from the Anglican Church. His residence, which he built in 1810, still stands on Pleasant Street, (pictured below). In his will of 1833, it is referenced as his "homestead" and gives the year of construction. William Foster served for a period as Deputy Sheriff in Guysborough; appointed in 1798 by W.T. Hierlihy. Later, Foster served as the village's jailor, and is listed as being a founding member of the Masonic Temple Lodge # 7 in Guysborough.

After William Foster's death, all of the property that his sons James and John inherited was seized by the Sheriff for debts owing. Clement Reynolds of Halifax purchased the properties at public auction; and as a merchant, may have been the Foster's business creditor. James died just six months after his father, on Christmas Day in 1833. The William Foster family is an excellent example of some of the early entrepreneurs that created a livelihood after starting with next to nothing, in the new settlement in Guysborough.

The William Foster homestead, Pleasant Street, Guysborough, 1810

Benjamin Godfrey 1739-1806

By Chris Cook

From the records that remain of Benjamin Godfrey, it appears that his time spent in the Guysborough area was quite brief. Further, the surname has now been lost in this part of the province, with the exception of the waterways Godfrey's Brook and Godfrey's Lake. Much of what is available to us today about Benjamin Godfrey comes from an article written about his mother (Elizabeth Hopkins Godfrey Tobey) by Lois Ware Thurston which appeared in the American Genealogist in 1991.

Benjamin Godfrey's father, also named Benjamin, and Elizabeth were living in Chatham Mass. at the time of his birth in 1740. By 1756, Benjamin Sr. had passed, and Elizabeth had married Nathanial Tobey. In 1762, Benjamin married Bethiah Atwood in Chatham, but in 1763 their first child's birth is recorded in Liverpool, N.S. There, he and Bethiah would have seven more children before her death in 1786.

By 1766 his mother and step-father Nathaniel Tobey followed Capt. Joseph Hadley to the Guysborough area and started a new life in Cook's Cove. After Bethiah's passing, Benjamin remained in Liverpool until 1790. Between 1786 and 1790, his two oldest daughters, Matthea and Deborah, moved to Cook's Cove to live with their grandmother. The other six children were sent back to Chatham, Mass., likely to live with Bethiah's family. Sadly, Matthea passed at the age of 21 in 1770.

Simeon Perkins, an early community leader of Liverpool, mentioned Benjamin Godfrey in his diary of 1803. He wrote: "Mr. Benjamin Godfrey, formerly an inhabitant of Town, and one of the first Settlers, who has been gone about 13 years, called upon me today. He lives at Chatham, Cape Cod, where he taught school." Being employed as a school teacher implies he was a learned individual and possessed an education greater than the common folk. Perhaps this explains why he did not just pack up and leave when his wife died, but instead sent his children elsewhere. He had a greater responsibility in the community and leaving was a difficult decision to make.

If he "called upon" Simeon Perkins in 1803, he must have been back in Nova Scotia. It appears from Jost's genealogical research that Benjamin's children had already by this point moved to the Guysborough area where their sister Deborah and grandmother Elizabeth were still residing. Shortly after the visit to Perkins, Benjamin must have made his way to Guysborough where his children, grandchildren, and mother were living. At this point Benjamin would have been in his early 60's. On May 26, 1806, the Christ Church Cemetery records state that Benjamin Godfrey had passed away at the age of 67.

John Grant ? - 1830

by Mark Haynes

Before coming to Guysborough in 1784, John Grant was listed on 8 June, 1783 as being a captain in the New York Militia based at Long Island.[4] Evidence exists showing he was a reasonably wealthy person for when he arrived in Guysborough he was accompanied by his personal slave Hannah, listed as being a Negro[5] plus Jack on loan from the Ass. Department of the Army and Navy.[6] In addition his wife Jane Grant also had a personal slave named Caser/Caesar, also listed as Negro, age 51.[7] Slaves were very expensive and only the upper echelons of society owned them. She also had a slave on loan from the Army, testament to the influence the Grants had. Accompanying them were children over ten years of age - J. A., James, Anne and Susannah. Children under ten were Betsy and Mary.

John Grant was given the usual land grants, one on the Milford Haven River, a town lot plus a large 600 acre back lot. This lot was the largest of all back lots handed out to Loyalist settlers who came to Guysborough indicating his position in society was esteemed. While common soldiers received a thirty acre riverside lot, he received a 216 acre one. He settled on lot #44 on the south side of the Milford Haven River just west of the Boylston bridge. His influence in the community was again reflected in 1787 when he became one of the first

---

[4] Christ Church Vestry Journal

[5] H. C. Hart, *History of the County of Guysborough,* Mika Pub. Co., Belleville, ON, 1975, p. 192

[6] June 1784 Muster list he arrived with wife, 6 children and having two Negro servants: Jack - belonging to the Ass. Dept. of the Army and Navy plus Hannah, his property.

[7] Harvey Amani Whitfield, *North to Bondage, Loyalist Slavery in the Maritimes,* UBC Press, 2016, p. 130

church officers, a vestryman, in the founding of Christ Church. As part of his duties he collected £5, 18 shillings and 6 pence by subscription for the expenses of moving Rev. Peter De La Roche and his family from Lunnenburg. In 1792 his income for tax purposes was listed in the Assessment Roll as above £40,[8] making him the second richest person in the community next to Nathan Hubbill.

The Grant family continued to grow with the arrival of three more children - William 1787, Jane 1789 and Julia 1792. Unfortunately this last birth was too much for Mrs. Grant and she died in childbirth. Being a widower with nine children, John needed another wife to care for his family. Lucky for him one Elizabeth Lyle became a widow in this same year when her husband James Lyle died. She too was of a wealthy family and was a good fit for him in the class system of the day. Having no will, in order for Mrs. Lyle to probate his estate, her husband's two slaves - Liberty and Sarah had to be registered as property in order for her to inherit them. In the Guysborough records is the following entry as proof of her husband's ownership:

Registered at Guysboro at 12 o'clock 9th November, 1793, at the request of David Martin, in book B., folio 415.

KNOWN ALL MEN BY THESE PRESENTS, that I, Matthew Lyle, Esq., late of Georgia but now of East Florida, for and in consideration of the sum of seventy pounds sterling to me in hand paid at and before the sealing and delivery of these presents by James Lyle of East Florida, the receipt whereof I do hereby acknowledge, have bargained and sold and by these presents do bargain and sell and deliver unto the said James Lyle three negroes to wit as follows: a negro man named Liberty and a wench and child named Sarah and Pegg. To have and to hold the said negroes unto the said James Lyle, his executors, administrators and assigns to his and their only proper use and behoof forever and I, the said Matthew Lyle, his executors and administrators the said bargained premises unto the said James Lyle his executors, administrators and assigns from and against all persons shall and will warrant and forever defend by these presents.

[8] H. C. Hart, Ibid, p. 232

60

*IN WITNESS WHEREOF I have hereunto set my hand and seal. Dated at
Saint Augustine on the 12th day of March, 1784 and in the 24th year of
His majesty's reign.*

*Signed, sealed and delivered in the presence of
Robert Sloane and Samuel Montgomery*

Matthew Lyle (Seal)

*Saint Augustine the 12th March, 1784. Received of James Lyle the just
and full sum of seventy pounds sterling it being in full payment of three
negroes named Liberty, Sarah and Pegg, which negroes was sold to
James Lyle by Matthew Lyle, Esq., which said three negroes, the said
Matthew Lyle have sold and delivered to the said James Lyle as witness
my hand.*

Matthew Lyle[9]

The deed shows James Lyle purchased his slaves at Saint Augustine in
East Florida (West Florida belonged to Spain at this time). Loyalists fled to East
Florida because it belonged to Britain. When it was agreed to give the area back
to Spain, they had to leave. The sum of money James Lyle paid for his slaves
was £70, quite a lot of money given a typical 30 acres riverside farm in
Guysborough was selling for around £4 at the time.

Elizabeth Lyle married John Grant on August 17, 1792. Between them
they had a total of twelve children and at least four slaves. There is no mention
of the slave Jack which Mr. Grant brought with him from New York. Perhaps he
was sold, died or had to be given back to the army. In the census of 1817 he is
still living on his original land grant. Those living on his property are listed as
one man over 50, 3 men between 16 and 50, 2 women and 2 girls. Total of 8. All
those listed in the census were of Scottish origin. Slaves were not listed

On May 7, in the same year he went into Thomas Cutler's store and
paid property taxes of 6 shillings for the year 1816. Then on July 1 he purchased
6 ½ pails of rum "for Road crew." This would be his contribution towards the
construction of a new road. A hint of how he earned a living comes in 1823
when he paid a debt to Cutler's store of £5 - 15 shillings with 11 ½ barrels of
mackerel. This indicates he was involved in the fishery. Later that same year he

---

[9] H. C. Hart, Ibid, p. 247

paid for a debt of £6 - 15 shillings from money received from the Provincial Treasurer. This suggests he was getting paid for some official government position he held.

Nothing else is known of John Grant until he died on June 2, 1830 and was interred in the graveyard of the church he helped establish. His age was not listed. As for his slaves Liberty, Sarah, Hannah and Caesar, they in all likelihood stayed slaves until they died. There are no records indicating they were buried in a Christian graveyard, as was the case of most slaves. Slavery ended in Nova Scotia by 1820.

62

Capt. William Grant 1749 – 1804

by: Chris Cook

Captain William Grant was a member of the 22nd Regiment during the American Revolution. Briefly, the 22nd regiment was sent to North America for service in the American Revolutionary War in 1775. Lieutenant Colonel James Abercrombie, commanding the regiment, embarked in advance of the rest of the regiment at the request of General Thomas Gage and arrived in Boston just before the Battle of Bunker Hill where he was killed in action. The regiment later evacuated from Boston to Halifax and then took part in the New York and New Jersey campaigns of 1776. The Battalion Companies participated in the Battle of Rhode Island in August 1778 and then returned to New York City in 1779; the bulk of the regiment remained there until the end of the War.

When William Grant got to Guysborough, because he was a ranking officer, his grant was significantly greater than the common settler. In addition to his town lot, in the North East division of the newly laid out town plan, he received a total of 450 acres of front and back lands. According to Guysborough historian A. C. Jost, the family retained a demit from the Regimental Lodge of the 22nd Regiment of Foot which he took with him to Port Mouton and then to Guysborough. It is now in the Public Archives of Nova Scotia. It reads:

> We, the Master, Wardens and Secretary of the Moriah Lodge no. 133 in His Majesty's 22nd Regiment of Foot on the Registry of Scotand do hereby certify that our trusty and well beloved brother William Grant was entered, passed and raised a master Mason, is a Past Master, and a Royal Arch Excellent Mason, and as such we recommend him to al regular Lodges and worthy brothers to whom these presents shall come. Given under our hands and the seal of our Lodge, 24th day of August 1783, Staten Island.

A typical soldier of the 22nd Regiment

Jost continued in stating that Captain Grant did not lose interest in Masonry after his removal to Guysborough, and was the first Master of old Temple Lodge, formed in Guysborough shortly after his arrival. He was married twice. His first wife was named Martha, and they had seven children. She died sometime between 1794 and 1801, and is likely also buried at Christ Church. However there are no records remaining of her interment. In June of 1801, it was recorded that Capt. Grant married a second time to Submit Leet, and they had two other children. One of William's grandsons was John Grant, the original proprietor of "Grant's Hotel" that stood for many years on the corner of Main and Broad Streets in Guysborough. Other descendants include George Grant who built many houses and public buildings in Guysborough and Laurier Grant, a community leader and recorder of 20th Century local events

Tyrus Hart 1773 – 1828

by Jamie Grant

Within a gated wrought-iron enclosure close to the southern stone wall of the cemetery, are two arched sandstone monuments to Tyrus Hart and Martha (Ingram) Hart (1782 – 1826). Tyrus Hart was born in Wallingford, Connecticut to parents Josiah and Lydia Hart. He lived here until 1787 when he accompanied his family to Manchester, where they settled on the Hallowell Grant. Lydia Hart died in 1809 at the age of 73 and was interred at Christ Church. At age 18, Tyrus acquired land of his own which he farmed until he was 27. He then sold his farm in Manchester and entered into mercantile business. He was the first in a long line of Hart-family merchants; a line which extended more than 200 years to the present day with Hart's General Store in Bolyston. In 1801 he married Martha Ingram, the sister of Armenia who had earlier married his brother Irad. Tyrus and Martha had 14 children over the next 20 years. At some time in the early 1820's he entered into a partnership with his son William in the growing community of Guysborough. At the same time he overssaw the construction of a new house for the family. It was here in 1826 that Martha died following the birth of their last child.

Not much is known about this business which was located on lower Main St. in Guysborough, other than it included trade with Newfoundland and that it prospered enough to accommodate his three oldest sons. It allowed for Tyrus to complete a large two and a half storey house on the corner of Church and Pleasant Streets. This house, known as the "Provincial Building" since its conversion in 1950 to office space, still stands as straight and true today as the day it was built.

Although Martha and Tyrus enjoyed success well above the norm for the time and place they were to be eclipsed by their remarkable family. Four of the 13 children who survived infancy, married into the prominent mercantile Whitman family of Canso; three were leading West Indian merchants, including Jairus, who was also president of the Bank of Nova Scotia, and one of the richest, most philanthropic men in the Province. Their three oldest sons (William, Joseph, and Tyrus Jr.), employed many locally in their shipyards, tannery, shoe factory, and aboard trading vessels. A Halifax newspaper article of 1900, outlined "A Honored Name" outlining the many accomplishment of the Harts, adds that "when they were all at home in Guysboro it was said that no finer looking family could be found in Canada."

Looks aside, accomplishments continued in the succeeding generations including leaders in the clergy, missionary work, business and the arts. Included among them were Raymond Massey, the leading actor of his time, and Vincent Massey, the first Canadian Governor General in our country's history.

Robert Hartshorne 1773 - 1851

by Dorothy Meyerhof

Robert Hartshorne, Equire, a member of the Cutler family compact of Guysborough, Nova Scotia, no doubt diligently carried out his many duties as Magistrate, Registrar of Deeds, Commissioner of Crown Lands, Commissioner of Schools, Commissioner for the Relief of Insolvent Debtors and Commissioner for Taking Special Bail. It has been noted that a man needed many positions to provide for a family as these positions often required little work and provided small recompense. Some members of these family compacts were bitterly resented however. One Guysborough resident with a number of these appointments was described as, "a regular porker, . . in receipt of 96 pounds sterling for the last sixty years, without performing the least service to the Country."

Robert was born into a Quaker family of businessmen and traders. Hartshorne ancestors settled in Monmouth Co., New Jersey about 1665. From Monmouth their movements can be traced through the Quaker Monthly Meetings to which they belonged, from Monmouth to Burlington, to Philadelphia, to Alexandria, VA, where Robert was born in 1775. Robert moved to New York, in 1806, remaining there amongst relatives until May 9, 1809 when he moved to Halifax.

In a letter to his sister Sarah, dated 9 May, 1809, Robert mentioned how very busy he had been preparing to travel to Halifax for an extended stay of between two and six months. Whether he returned to the United States after this visit, or if this represented his permanent move to Halifax, is not known. The New York Monthly Meeting of Quakers disowned him on 7 February 1817, as by this time he had been in Halifax, NS, for some years and had married outside the Quaker faith.

Robert sought to become a British subject in February 1812. A document (memorial) he submitted in support of his request, noted he was born in Virginia and "that he came from the United States upwards of two years ago, and hath since been by presumption constantly residing at Dartmouth, . . . where he hath been concerned with Mess. Hartshorne and Tremain in a Grist Mill and an Extensive Bakery of Hard Bread." Several days later, on 12 February 1812, he was one of many who signed a Declaration of Allegiance to the British Crown, five months before the United States ignited the War of 1812 by declaring war on Great Britain.

The *Mr. Hartshorne* of the Dartmouth Grist Mill and Bakery, with whom Robert worked, was Lawrence Hartshorne, first cousin of Robert's father William. Lawrence would have been a good person to know. He was a favourite of Lieutenant Governor John Wentworth and one of the leading business men of the province with interests in manufacturing, mining and banking. As an MLA, MLC and a pal of governor Wentworth (who was often in his debt), he also possessed major political power.

Robert became even more involved in the business life of the Halifax-Dartmouth area. In addition to his association with the Hartshorne/Tremaine Grist Mill and Bakery in Dartmouth, by 1813 he was also engaged in a general store and trade business with Richard and James Tremaine, sons of Lawrence Sr.'s partner Jonathan Tremaine. In March 1814, Robert Hartshorne was one of four men, the others being Thomas Kegan (surgeon), James Lowrie (ship's surgeon) and Michael Bennett, who together received a crown grant of land totalling two thousand acres. Robert's share was five hundred acres in the district of Musquedoboit. In May of the same year, he was appointed Trustee of a school established in Dartmouth.

It was likely through the social circles of Lawrence Hartshorne that Robert met his wife Harriet Elizabeth (Cutler) Ballaine. Harriet's father, Thomas Cutler, like Lawrence, was a Loyalist refugee in the 1783 exodus from New York. Although not part of the exalted political circles Lawrence inhabited in Halifax, Thomas was none-the-less an important person in Guysborough, where he was known as *King* Cutler and it was said that "if anything took place in the county

[Sydney] in which *King* Cutler was not interested or in someway involved, one may be sure it was of very minor importance."

Thomas and Lawrence may have met as members of the Legislative Assembly of Nova Scotia where they served at the same time. Harriet Cutler had married John Ballaine on 24 December 1806, a businessman from Arichat, Cape Breton, who was elected to the Legislative Assembly in 1811. Tragically he drowned in Halifax Harbour on 10 April 1812. Exactly how and when Robert was introduced to the young widow is not known, however, the two were wed in her home town of Guysborough, Sydney Co. in April or May of 1816 when Robert was 43. In July of that year, he along with William Allen, John B. Coleman, Charles Reeves and Seth Coleman all of Dartmouth, received a grant of three acres, three roods and one perch (equivalent to slightly more than 3 3/4 acres) in the Town of Dartmouth and Harbour of Halifax including six town lots and four water lots. Presumably this grant would have provided a home for him and his new bride. Two of their children were born during their time in Dartmouth, Harriet in December 1816 and William in December 1819.

Thomas Cutler played a key role in his son-in-law's integration into the life of Guysborough. On 1 January 1821, he endowed the couple with forty acres of land on Smith's Point (now the Belmont) that he had received as a grant in 1813. On the same day Thomas gave Robert this land, Robert became President of the Manchester and Guysborough Farmers' Society. According to the Secretary of the Society, Guysborough was in the process of switching from a sole reliance on fishing to farming as a mainstay of the economy.

From his life as a trader, he settled successfully into farming. It is possible he was influenced by his cousin Lawrence Hartshorne, Sr. who "was active in agricultural improvements as the treasurer of a pioneering agricultural society and [was] the owner of a model farm in Cole Harbour." Robert's own farm management seems to have been exemplary as described by one of his grandsons:

> There were always three men and a boy for field work, and
> two women and a girl in the house. He was familiar with the
> plantation life of the south, and for his day, was a scientific farmer. He
> had a very fine apple and plum orchard of imported trees. He was
> constantly getting seeds from the United States and always developed
> his own potatoes from the seed-balls. He put up a grist and carding

*mill on his property ... importing his millwright, and blacksmith. . . .
Butter and cheese making were of course, carried on – also distilling of
roses, the making of wines, bay-berry candles, in fact everything
possible to a selfcontained [sic] property. He kept his flock of sheep up
to 200 – six always fattening in a farmyard pen.*

*At nine p.m. he went into the kitchen to give the men orders
for the morning. Before breakfast, in season, he worked for an hour or
two in the kitchen-garden – always a showplace. After breakfast, he
rode over the place to superintend and direct. He bred his own horses
– always a saddler for his daughter. A matched pair of drivers was
bought by the Governor of the Province. He kept the open house of the
day, visiting gentlemen going there as a matter of course.*

Robert was active in many aspects of the social and commercial life of
Guysborough. Although he clearly paid attention to his farming, he did not give
up trading entirely. In 1829 he became the owner of the schooner *Nancy*,
registered in Sydney. The Nancy had a crew of 5 and Robert was listed as a
Merchant. In this he joined with his father-in-law who also owned a schooner,
the *Alligator*, built in 1818. Robert continued his interest in education and in
1825 was chosen one of three school trustees for Guysborough, along with Rev.
James Grant and Wentworth Taylor. His interest in education extended to the
education of his daughters. Both the eldest and youngest of his daughters,
Harriet and Lucy, respectively, spent a year in Halifax completing their
education. In addition to managing the farm and mill, trading, and fulfilling his
public duties, Robert also engaged in numerous land transactions including
providing mortgages. He joined other land owners in Guysborough who signed
a petition to have roads in the county improved.

Post Card showing the Hartshorne home at the left on the
Belmont. (Nova Scotia Archives, Halifax, NS)

Robert was also active in the religious and moral life of the
community. Shortly after arriving in Guysborough he rented the Governor's
pew in Christ Church. According to his grandson, William S. H. Morris:

> [He] *was a stern opponent of the prevailing intemperance. He
> never allowed his men rum – as was the custom; but beer was
> regularly brewed, and the men filled their small keg every morning to
> take to the fields. He was much criticized and told that he would not
> get men to work for him, but he always had good men, and in hay and
> harvest time his work went steadily on, while in other fields the men
> would be fighting at midafternoon. Together with Wentworth Taylor,
> Esq. he organized in Guysborough what was probably the first
> Temperance Society in Nova Scotia..*

In a letter to his sister in Virginia on 29 May, 1831, he remarks, "for
you perhaps will be surprised to know that I have lately be appointed one of the
judges of our Court of Common Pleas for the County of Sydney, but my
principal business is attending to a large farm I got from my Father-in-Law
Cutler with a small lot with a Mill attached to it, here my dear Sister will no
doubt say her Brother is more at home or in his proper element than sitting on

the Judges Bench of a court of Justice and perhaps she will not be far wrong, be that as it may, he assured it was not an office of my seeking"

His position as a magistrate was soon put to the test. Robert was one of the judges called on to deal with the miscreants in the Canso riots of October 1833. The riots were the culmination of events escalating from the mischievous docking of a horse's tail, to vicious assaults, riots, arrests and finally claims that Protestants were persecuting Catholics. Threats received from Father James Grant, a catholic priest, so concerned Robert and others involved with bringing the perpetrators to justice that they wrote to Sir Rupert D. George, Bart. provincial Secretary with copies of the threatening letters requesting protection for themselves and other residents of Guysborough and Canso. The Magistrates had been told they would be ". . . shot like ducks . . ." if they continued to pursue those involved. With sufficient manpower the wrongdoers were brought to justice. By January 1834 the affair had been mostly settled, although Robert wrote to Martin Wilkins, Crown Attorney for the affair, that he didn't think, ". . . the Judge [was] done with the trouble growing out of the late proceedings . . . but a number . . . are .. . pleased with the punishment of these vagabonds."

Robert and Harriet raised a flourishing family of two boys and four girls in Guysborough; Harriet Ann (1816), William Henry (1819), Sophia Caroline (1821), Lawrence (1823), Elizabeth and Lucy (1828). In 1838 Robert's young family began to marry. Harriet Ann was the first, marrying local Anglican clergyman, Rev. Charles Jessen Shreve, son of Rev. Thomas Shreve late of Parrsboro and Lunenburg. Sophia Caroline was the second daughter to marry in October 1846. Her spouse was James E. Cutler a merchant (not closely related to her grandfather Thomas Cutler).

Harriet Hartshorne died in February, 1847 She had lived to see two daughters married and to celebrate the arrival of four grandchildren born to her daughter Harriet and Charles J. Shreve. A year after his wife died, Robert took his youngest daughter Lucy to stay with her aunts and uncles in Virginia and Pennsylvania. His letter to her on his return gives a quick overview of the situation in Guysborough compared to what he saw in Baltimore:

> After I left you, I spent the next day at Baltimore at E. Stablers
> and was at the fair and cattle show plowing match and exhibit on
> Tools . . . Our country and the county of Sydney are more destitute

than I ever knew them, no potatoes or grain in the latter and but little in the former. It is quite melancholy after leaving so beautiful a country . . . I have just returned home from our Agricultural meeting . . . it looked very small after seeing that at Baltimore" [and a comment on the state of affairs in his own household] *. . . They have been getting along so well that I am now sorry that I did not stay all winter. William is a better manager than I expected . . . My friends here tell me I look some years younger than when I left home. This is encouragement to go again but at my time of life I can hardly expect a continuance of so good health..*

The Hartshorne Mill. (*Historic Guysborough,* John M. Grant, 2004)

His dismal prediction was to prove true. Four years later, on Saturday, 22 March, 1851, Robert died at the age of 77. In the three decades since his arrival from Dartmouth, he had played a prominent part in establishing Guysborough's, now largely forgotten, "Golden Age". He and Harriet lay under a large grey sandstone table monument within a wrought Iron enclosure close to the gate of Christ Church cemetery.

Just less than a year later there were two deaths in the Hartshorne family in quick succession. Harriet Ann Shreve, Robert's eldest daughter died on Thursday 13 March, 1851 after a short illness, only five months after the birth of her

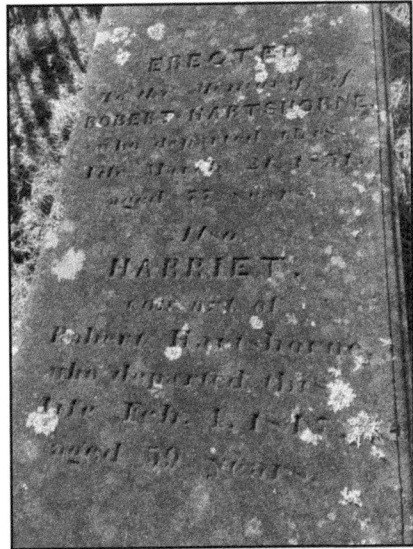

Harriet and Robert Hartshorne's table style monument in Christ Church cemetery.

youngest son Richmond Uniacke Shreve. One week later, on Saturday 22 March, Robert died. Both deaths may have been due to the influenza epidemic that swept North America in 1850 - 1851, although Robert had also been suffering from asthma for some time. His mortal remains and those of his wife Harriet lie beneath a large sandstone table style monument in Christ Church Cemetery.

Abridged from "Robert Hartshorne" by Dorothy Mayerhof. The original unpublished paper is housed at the Old Court House Museum, Guysborough, NS.

Hannah Hawkins ? - 1814

by Mark Haynes

How do we find out who Hannah Hawkins was when the only clue as to her existence is an entry in Christ Church cemetery register which reads "Hannah Hawkins (negroed), died Nov. 1, buried Nov. 2, 1814". That is the only evidence in the entire world indicating anyone by that name ever existed. None-the-less it is possible to conjecture who she might be. For instance, her last name is Hawkins, would that be a married name or a maiden name? If it is a maiden name then due to her African-American heritage it would be a name derived from a slave owner. In addition to that she died in Guysborough. The vast majority of African-Americans who came to Guysborough at that time were listed in the Book of Negroes. They escaped slavery during the American Revolution and shipped out of New York in 1783 to Port Mouton, Nova Scotia. Then due to the poor location of the town and a fire, moved on to Guysborough in 1784.

So in all likelihood she would have come to Guysborough as part of that migration. There is no one by the name of Hannah Hawkins listed in the Book of Negroes though. The trick to finding out who she might be is by searching for any females with the first name Hannah in this book. It turns out there were six females by that name, five of them with last names who were accompanied by men. Hence it is assumed they were with their husbands. The sixth person is a Hannah Ellis who was single, twenty years old and described as a stout wench who left her enslaver, William Ellis of South Carolina, around 1778. If she was the one who ended up with the last name Hawkins, it is fair to conclude she married someone of African-American decent with that last name.

There is only one single Afro-American man in the Book of Negroes who went to Guysborough with the last name of Hawkins, and that is Sam Hawkins. He is listed as being 26 years of age, arriving in Port Mouton in 1783. According to the Book of Negroes he was described as a stout fellow who was with the Wagon Master General Department. Formerly a slave to John Hawkins of Rye, New England, he took his masters last name and kept it after he ran away in 1779.

When these freed slaves got to Guysborough there was a muster list made of those who received rations from the British Government to help them survive until they were self sufficient. They received hoes, shovels, axes, etc., the same as white Loyalist settlers. Samuel Hawkins' name appears on this list, so we know he moved on to Guysborough from Port Mouton. He is not listed as being with anyone, and the muster list is quite detailed. There is no Hannah Ellis on the list so it appears she either died in Port Mouton or went somewhere else like Digby, Nova Scotia or New Brunswick where a few Loyalists went instead of Guysborough. So it is doubtful she is the one who married Samuel Hawkins.

There is however one lady named Hannah on the muster list and that is Hannah Pierce, but she is not in the Book of Negroes so she didn't come up from Port Mouton. So where did she come from? To get her name on the muster list means she had to be a freed slave. Most likely she came up with the St. Augustine Loyalists who arrived from Florida in the fall of 1784. They were given land out by St. Francis Harbour and along the Straits of Canso because all the land around Guysborough was taken. More than likely, if she came with this group, she would be alone for few persons of African-American descent came with them unless they were indentured servants. Seeing as she would never get a land grant there due to her colour, she probably went to Guysborough hearing there was a group of freed ex slaves gathered there. This was at 'Niggertown Hill,' an area just behind the Cutler Estate by Cutler's Cove. They were waiting to get land grants promised to them. There is also the slim possibility she landed in Country Harbour and walked overland up to Guysborough, but the St. Augustine Loyalist theory is more probable due to it being closer.

The next step in figuring out who she might be is to look at the grants of those Afro-Americans who got land in Tracadie in 1787. Everyone on the muster list got land except for Hannah Pierce who is never heard from again. Is this because her last name changed? In 1803 a woman by the name of Hannah Hawkins sold a lot of land in Tracadie. Seeing as no one by this name received a grant there, the only way she could come into ownership of a lot of land was if she married someone with that last name and he died. Consequently she would have inherited it. This shows Samuel Hawkins got married sometime between 1787, when we know he was single and received a lot in Tracadie, and 1803 when a lady with his last name sold it. As there was only one lady of African-

American descent in the area who was single and had the first name Hannah, this could only be Hannah Pierce.

Unfortunately there are no church records surviving from the early days in Tracadie East or Upper Big Tracadie until 1822 when a Baptist Church was built there. Even the pioneer cemetery there has no grave markers, so all we can do is conjecture. It is rational to presume on the death of her husband, and maybe children too, as there are no records of children of African-American descent with the last name Hawkins, she sold the lot and moved to Guysborough to get a job as a servant. Though she died in 1814 and was buried in Christ Church cemetery, a census done in 1817 lists 27 black servants in the village of Guysborough in that year, so there were plenty of servant jobs. In the same census is listed the names of all black persons living in Tracadie and the last name Hawkins is not amongst them. It would be nice if the Hannah which Samuel Hawkins married had been Hannah Ellis who was in the Book of Negroes, then we would know her age and where she came from as it is always listed in the book. Unfortunately Hannah Pierce was not in the book and hence we will never know when she was born or where she originated from in the thirteen colonies other than it was somewhere near Charlestown, South Carolina where the St. Augustine loyalists originated. After two hundred years this is all that is known about Hannah Hawkins.

Henry Inch   1797 - 1829

by Jamie Grant

Henry Inch was born in Londonderry, Ireland, and in his petition for land in 1821 says he emigrated from Ireland to Guysborough "four years ago and was twenty four years of age". Though he presented himself as a physician, there is no record of his attending any medical school in Ireland, Scotland or England. It seems more likely he was trained as an apothecary. In a Supreme Court case in Guysborough, October 30, 1819, he was charged with being indebted for a large consignment of pharmaceuticals purchased on July 28, 1817 when he seems to have established his office/drug store on Queen Street.

He next appears in the records in an unusual document for the time, a pre-nuptial agreement. It reads as follows:

> *Articles of Agreement of two parts . . . between Henry Inch of Guysborough, Nova Scotia of the first part and Mary Paterson of aforesaid place (Daughter of the late William Nixon) of the second part as followeth: Whereas a marriage is shortly intended to take place between the above named Henry Inch and Mary Paterson and whereas the said Henry Inch firmly agrees and binds himself on this Twenty eighth Day of March in the year of our Lord one thousand eight hundred and twenty, that providing the said Mary Paterson makes good her promise of marriage to him as agreed . . . that the said Henry Inch for himself heirs, administrators and assigns both firmly bind himself by this instrument of writing to said Mary Paterson her heirs, administrators and assigns that whatever property she may now possess, be it house, furniture, plate, cattle, debts, mortgages, deeds or property of whatever sort or kind, to reserve all claim to after the said Mary Paterson shall become his wife, and that it shall be to her own use and disposal in whatever way she may think proper and that she may have power to will, sell or dispose of said property in any way she may think proper for her own benefit and advantage. In witness*

whereof the aforesaid Parties to those present have hereby set their hands and seals the day and date above mentioned.

Mary Paterson did "make good her promise of marriage to him" as the Halifax Journal reported on April 17, 1820. He was twenty-three, she forty-six. Mary Paterson was the daughter of William Nixon, an early merchant of Guysborough and the widow of Dr. John Paterson, a naval surgeon of Bermuda who died in August, 1818. She seems to have returned from Bermuda to Guysborough, perhaps to care for her aging mother who died the following year. While it is impossible to enter the minds of those long dead, the facts surrounding this May - September marriage are clear. A young immigrant facing debtors prison marries the childless widow of a naval officer who has just inherited the estate of her once prosperous parents and is twice her husbands age. It seems likely the pre-nuptial agreement was precipitated, at least in part, by Inch's debts.

For the next few years he seems to have prospered, winning approval of the town's elite and avoiding debt despite the typically low income common to doctors of the day. In 1823 we learn some personal knowledge of him when he went into Thomas Cutler's store and purchased a handkerchief, some snuff and a Scottish Bonnet, also known as a Tam O' Shanter. This does suggest he may have been a bit of a *dandy*,

Typical Scottish Bonnet or Tam O' Shanter (photo courtesy of Etsy).

as they would have said in those days.

Also in 1823 Dr. William Cantrell, a graduate of Trinity College, Dublin, set up a competing practice which would have eaten into Inch's already meagre income. There may have been other factors as well, but in any event over the next four years properties belonging to his wife were sold and he seems to have lost favour with the influential.

The downward spiral of his fortune would only accelerate, for the next mention of him is "Henry Inch of Guysborough, committed to the goal in Guysboro on January 27, 1829". Worse was to come; the very next night he drew his final breath. The remarkably sparse records of the day reveal neither the charge against him nor the circumstances under which he left the jail. But, by some means , he did get out since his frozen corpse was discovered early in the morning of January 29, 1829 on the Market Square close to his residence. He had been "run through with a sword".

The records again fail to convey just how the officials responded, but, it is clear that two members of the prominent Marshall family faced judgement by a court presided over by six Justices, three of whom could not be considered impartial. One, Joseph Marshall, was the father of one and grandfather of the other accused. A second was connected by marriage to both and the third was a close neighbour of both the accused and the victim. The actual offence with which the accused was charged was not recorded but no conviction resulted. An earlier inquest conducted by the third Justice, John Newton, found Inch had died by a "visitation from God."

The second attempt at a trial occurred within the year in a new venue and with two additional accused. The court records payment to the deputy sheriff for transporting James H Marshall, James Marshall, James Kennedy, and George English from Guysborough to the jail in Antigonish. Again the charges against them were not recorded nor any explanation of why the Marshalls faced a second rial or of why the other two were added to the docket. No record of the trial survives but tradition holds that none of the witnesses gave evidence and that the Crown's case collapsed. Guysborough historian A. C. Jost was on safe ground with his conclusion that, "The whole story of the events leading up to the doctor's death has never been made known." The same could be said of the related "events" following the demise.

Henry Inch's body was laid to rest in a forgotten plot at Christ Church Cemetery unmarked by a tombstone. Mrs. Mary Inch disappeared from the records. No account of her death has been found in Canada, the US or Bermuda, adding yet another layer of mystery to the puzzle.

Editor's note: This story is abridged from a longer account available at the Old Court Hose Museum

Robert Kay 1769 - 1850

by Jamie Grant

From Mrs. H. C. Hart's *History of the County of Guysborough*, we lean that Robert Kay was a "noted musician" and highly regarded music teacher who did much to improve local musical performances in church and for "entertainments". Both he and his wife, Marjory, were Scottish born and lived at the northern edge of the town, "high on a hill where Church St. becomes the old road to Antigonish", and called their residence Windygow. It seems they had migrated from Britain directly to Guysborough in 1824 when Robert was 54 and Marjory 32. This date is based on Dr. George Buckley's 1907 record of their son's (Robert Cutler Kay Jr.) death. It states that he was born on the immigrant ship which brought them and that he was aged 83 when he died. This explains the absence of a Nova Scotia birth record but raises other questions. Did the Kays already know Robert Cutler before arrival and gave their son's middle name in honour of him or did they add Cutler to his name later?

In any event, their origins and the circumstances surrounding their relocation has led to a great deal of rumour and speculation among the curious. Mrs. Hart, who would have known them in her youth, was silent on the subject but the tittle-tattle must have excited Victorian imaginations. In *As I Remember It*, Mrs. Hilda Cox reminisced in 1964 about the Kays;

> *I wish I knew the true story of Bob Kay (Robert Junior). I don't remember seeing him, for in my young days he lived alone and probably never came into town. On Sunday afternoon, if we took a walk on the old road over the hill, we would see Mr. Burton Jost walking down, carrying papers to Bob Kay, for Bob was a remittance man, and money was sent from England for his needs - evidently via Mr. Jost. The old story is that his mother (Marjorie) was an English lady, connected in some way with Lord Russell's family, and that she ran away with the coachman or gardener or some other employee of the family (Robert Kay Sr.). . . . After his death, Mrs. Kay lived with*

(her son) Bob in the little grey house. The little grey house has been gone for years.

The Lord Russell referred to was twice the Prime Minister of Great Britain. He owned an estate of 16,000 acres and was related to many other leading aristocratic families. He and a number of relatives attended the University of Edinburgh as had the then Lieutenant Governor of Nova Scotia, Sir James Kent. Might Kent have known Lord Russell and involved Robert Cutler in a conspiracy to hide the Kays in remote Guysborough to cover up a Russell family scandal? James Kent was familiar with Guysborough, having visited in 1822 and was well acquainted with Cutler who had hosted him while he was here.

Perhaps, but there is little doubt that someone was supporting Bob Kay. On the various censuses his occupation is either listed as being a "gentleman" or is left out. Since "gentleman" meant a man of independent means and not gainfully employed, it's likely he never worked a day in his life. His father died at age eighty-one in 1850 and his mother in 1872. Surely Robert Senior's earnings as a music teacher could not have supported Marjory for twenty-two years after his death and his son Bob for another fifty-seven. Bob was also reclusive and considered eccentric.

The Russells also tended to be eccentric. Those of the 20th Century included a recluse and one so devoted to his huge collection of parrots that he completely ignored everything else including his son who didn't attend school and was sixteen years old before he realized he was the heir of the estate. When the son took over the estate, it was so indebted that he turned it into a sort of amusement park to the horror of his fellow aristocrats. Burtrum Russell, the brilliant mathematician and philosopher, was an intellectual giant but many of his views were hardly main stream.

Lastly, if Marjory did run away with some employee of the family, might it have been her music teacher? In the novels of the day noble women's affections were often won by dancing masters or music teachers. This might explain Robert Kays "noted" musical accomplishments.

So had Robert Kay - coachman, gardener or music teacher, run off with an aristocratic lady or had her family sent them away to avoid scandal? The answers to these mysteries lie buried with the Kays beneath a lonely old grey gravestone in Christ Church Cemetery and we can only wonder.

82

Gravestone of Robert Kay

Andrew Leet   1731 - 1808

by Jamie Grant

Andrew Leet was a successful farmer in Guildford, Connecticut, where he was born 6 November, 1731 and where his family had lived since its founding in 1639. His great grandfather, William Leete (1613 - 1683), was a Puritan who left England because of his religious principles and was later Governor of both New Haven and Connecticut colonies. Andrew married Esther Blatchy, 12 May, 1763; they divorced 28 August, 1769.

About this time Benjamin Hallowell of Boston was recruiting settlers for his 20,000 acre land grant in present day Manchester, Nova Scotia and it seems Leet may have been one of those considering taking up his offer. It is known that several men from his area visited Hallowell's grant to assess the prospects there in June, 1773 and returned with hopes of relocating. If Leet was a member of this group he didn't linger there long since he was in Guilford on 7 October, 1773 when he married Submit Cockard, a divorcee with one daughter, Cassandra. If he had planned to emigrate, he must have changed his mind for as well as remarrying, he was soon buying more farmland in Guilford.

Whatever his plans, the turmoil that developed into the civil war, known as the American War of Independence, soon intruded completely disrupting the life he had always known. In a series of petitions to the Connecticut General Assembly, he made his position clear. His "political loyalty" was to the King and he would not take up arms against him nor would he fight against his neighbours who were "engaged" against him, though he believes their cause ill advised. Rather, he would "choose to live peaceably with all men enjoying the Liberty of his own conscience".

He first expressed his willingness on 26 February, 1778 to leave the Sates if it was felt his presence posed a danger to their cause. He also pointed out to the Assembly that both General Washington's orders and the Congress exempted conscientious objectors from army service and that he would continue to obey all laws and pay his taxes. In a later petition he complained that his cattle and goods to the value of £62 had been commandeered by the

State and that he had been jailed for no crime and charged £15 for his keep. He thought he was being made an example of and again "begged leave to remove from the State." Regardless, no restitution was made. It was not until May, 1786 he was able to leave after selling most of his land. His married son remained in Connecticut and Andrew never saw him again.

About the end of the month he sailed with Captain David Scranton and sixteen other families for Manchester where he acquired a 150 acre lot on the Hallowell Grant. However he didn't settle there for on August 14th he purchased 600 acres on the north side of the Milford Haven River from Lieutenant Angus MacDonald for £190 and spent the rest of his life on the property. At 55 years of age he was starting over in a new land but he had assets most of his neighbours lacked. The skill sets both he and Submit brought ideally suited their new situation, his half grown sons could help and he had money while few others did not. The family prospered, married and lived near by with the homestead remaining in the family for almost two-hundred years. Andrew continued accumulating land until, by the time of his death, he owned 1,328 acres and according to his will, no debts.

One wonders if, when the old man was writing his will, he reflected on the stance he took back in Connecticut thirty years before. He had chosen principle over pragmatism and like his great grandfather William, 140 years earlier, had consequently become an exile. Both had been governed by the dictates of conscience as they believed God demanded. Submit died first on 4 October, 1804 and Andrew four years later on 16 February, 1808. Both were laid to rest in Christ Church Cemetery among others who shared their "political loyalties".

Murdoch MacLean 1807 - 1865

by Colin Harding

      Born on March 18, 1807 in Kingairloch, Scotland, Murdoch MacLean emigrated to Pictou, NS with his family in 1812. He married Elizabeth Mary Armstrong Cutler on January 7, 1839, and died on April 4, 1865. There is no gravestone remaining to mark his place of burial in Christ Church cemetery, however one would assume it would have been near the Cutler family plot. Elizabeth died on July 26, 1890, and is buried at Arichat ,Nova Scotia. Murdoch was educated at Pictou Academy and was a law apprentice with his uncle, James Skinner. He served as High Sheriff of Guysborough County, Nova Scotia, from 1836 to 1863. He was the 17th ancestral Chieftain of Clan MacLean of Kingairloch, Scotland. Two of his sons were future Kingairloch Chieftains, Kenneth John – 18th Chieftain, and Robert Cutler, 19th Chieftain, and a third son, Albert William, was the father of William Edward, 20th Chieftain. A fourth son was Norman Campbell MacLean. Kenneth tragically drowned at the age of 29 near Pictou, explaining why the Chieftainship went to his brother Robert. Robert immigrated to Freeport Maine in 1870.

      As a young boy, Murdoch's voyage from Scotland to Pictou NS was indeed hair-raising. Family history tells us that when Murdoch's father, Hector MacLean, inherited the title of Clan Chieftain from his brother, he "found the estate in debt". The brother was a gambler, and as a result was 10,000GBP in debt, having "gambled away his inheritance and lost the place at the turn of a card in Almanac's Club in London". As a result, in order to pay off the debt, Hector was forced to sell the entire Kingairloch estate in 1803 to James Forbes of Hutton Hall, Essex, who took possession in 1812. With the proceeds he bought a ship, and he and his family, and the clan of approximately 500 people emigrated to Pictou, NS. However, the ship that was loaded with all the family's belongings, struck a ledge going through the Strait of Canso and sank with the loss of most of the family's belongings. He later partnered with his brother-in-law, Colonel Simon Fraser, as a merchant on Deacon's Wharf and built a house at 76 Front St, Pictou, NS that is still there today. However, in reference to the loss of the family's belongings in the ship wreck, in a letter from Sir James MacLean, the Clan's silver and papers did survive. But in a quirk of family history for reasons unknown, upon the death of Murdoch's mother, Elizabeth, she bypassed Murdoch and left to her younger son, Simon, "all my furniture, silver place, family documents, moveables, and all my personnel property of whatever description". Simon was apparently Elizabeth's favoured son. Simon had one son, John Fraser MacLean, who died unmarried during the American Civil War. He also had two daughters, Frances and Christina. For those artifacts that did survive, they were probably passed down the families of Simon's two sisters. This would further explain why there are so few Kingairloch MacLean artifacts, etc. that have survived. Simon declared bankruptcy in 1851,went to the gold fields in Nerrigundah, Australia, without his family, and died there in 1868.

According to the 1871 Census, Murdock's widow, Elizabeth, was 60 years old and residing in Guysborough. Living with her were their children Kenneth, aged 26 (occupation: seaman), William, aged 23 (occupation: baker), Elizabeth, aged 27 (occupation: seamstress), Norman, aged 20 (occupation: courier), and their 17 year old son Frances.

Hector Murdock MacLean

Joseph Marshall 1755 - 1847

by Judith Tullock

Joseph Marshall was as a Judge, Justice of the Peace, militia officer, politician, and farmer; b. circa. 1755 in Glenkeen, Northern Ireland, fourth child of Joseph Marshall and Mary (Hagan?); m. Margaret —, probably in Georgia before 1783, and they had three sons; d. 3 June 1847 at his home in Guysborough, N.S.

Joseph Marshall was a boy of 13 in 1769 when his family immigrated to Georgia. They settled on the Ogeechee River, west of Savannah. Family tradition recounts that the Marshalls moved to British controlled territory in West Florida at the outbreak of the American revolution. Along with several of his brothers, Marshall joined the loyalist forces, and in April 1779 he was appointed lieutenant-colonel of a Georgia militia regiment. In May 1780 he was commissioned captain in the Carolina King's Rangers, a loyalist corps raised in the Floridas but composed principally of Georgians. The Rangers fought through the bitter southern campaign and were finally withdrawn to St. Augustine (Fla), the last British foothold in the south. Most of the corps, as well as veterans of two other Carolina regiments, were evacuated with their families to Halifax in October 1783. They were disbanded there early in November and, despite the onset of winter, were then transported along the eastern shore to Country Harbour, where the loyalist township of Stormont was surveyed the following spring.

The inhospitable, although scenic, terrain of Country Harbour presented formidable difficulties for the new settlers, and within a few years many had left in search of brighter economic prospects elsewhere. Although Marshall had been granted 1,100 acres of land at Country Harbour, he too moved, to the more sheltered shores of Chedabucto Bay. He purchased land on the east side of Guysborough Harbour early in 1795 and developed a substantial property, called Glenkeen after his birthplace.

Marshall played a prominent role in the Guysborough area throughout his long life. He was
appointed a justice of the peace

in May 1784 and served as a judge of the Inferior Court of Common Pleas from 1799 until the court's abolition in 1841. One of the most senior loyalist officers to settle in Guysborough, he was commissioned a major in the Sydney County militia in 1794, although he does not appear to have served, possibly being disgruntled at the appointment of the less experienced but more influential Thomas Cutler as lieutenant-colonel. In 1808, when the county regiment was divided in two, Marshall was appointed lieutenant-colonel of the 10th (Dorchester) Battalion with Cutler's son, Robert Molleson, becoming lieutenant-colonel of

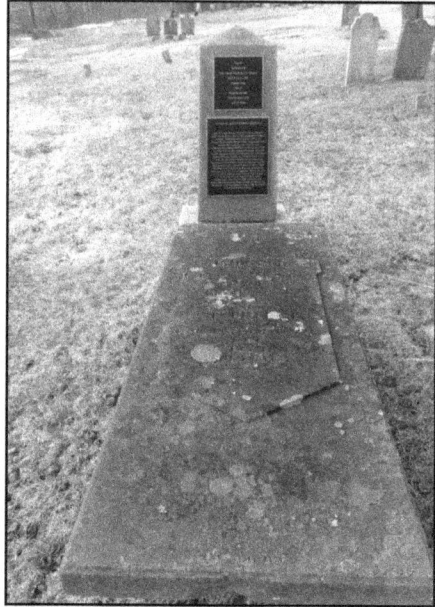

Capt. Joseph and Margaret Marshall gravestone and new monument.

the 19th (Guysborough) Battalion.

Marshall also represented Sydney County in the House of Assembly for two terms, the first of three generations of his family to serve in the legislature. He was elected in February 1800, too late to attend the first meeting, but he took his seat at the spring session of 1801. Despite the problems of travelling from one of the most isolated areas of Nova Scotia, Marshall was in regular attendance through the heated debates of the eighth assembly. He served on a number of committees, principally those dealing with road appropriations, and usually voted with William Cottnam Tonge's "country party." Re-elected in 1806, Marshall again was usually found among Tonge's supporters. He endorsed, for example, Tonge's attempt to eliminate complimentary references from the assembly's address to the retiring lieutenant governor Sir John Wentworth.

Marshall did not attend the 1811 legislative session and planned to retire in favour of his son John George when an election was called that autumn. The younger Marshall and another new candidate, John Ballaine, were to stand unopposed but at the last moment one of the former members, John Cunningham, decided to run. Joseph Marshall, Cunningham, and Ballaine then met and agreed that in order to avoid the expense of a contested election the two previous members would be acclaimed. However, John George, who had not been at the meeting and was irritated at its outcome, determined to stand. His father then willingly withdrew to help with the younger man's ultimately successful campaign in the contested election that ensued.

Unlike many Guysborough residents, Marshall was primarily a farmer, and in 1819 he served on the first executive of the Guysborough and Manchester Farmer Society. He exemplified the many loyalists of middle rank who became community leaders in their new homes. Indeed, as a southerner, he was more representative of Nova Scotia loyalists than traditionally has been acknowledged, since analysis of their origins indicates that as many as 30 per cent were from the southern colonies. One of the founders of what is now Guysborough County, Marshall was the progenitor of a family of prosperous farmers and merchants who developed a tradition of public service.

Captain Joseph Marshall

The McColl Family

Duncan, Caroline, Archibald, Wallace, Malcolm, Robert and Elizabeth

by Dr. Anita Foley

Duncan McColl married into Guysborough's most prominent family of the first half of the 1800's, the Cutlers. According to Alan Wilson's book, *Highland Shepherd*, McColl was a bright young man from Argyllshire, Scotland who profited from his older brother's connections as aide-de-camp to the Lieutenant Governor in Halifax, and therefore won the Guysborough Collector of Customs office. Though it is uncertain as to when he first came to Guysborough, he married Caroline Cutler, the daughter of 'King' Thomas Cutler, on November 16, 1814. In 1821 he bought a large house at the corner of Pleasant and Main Street in Guysborough, which had been built by a Dr. Stickles. It is known that McColl was one of the founders of Temple Lodge # 7 in Guysborough, one of the earliest Masonic Lodges outside of Halifax in 1785.

Duncan and Caroline McColl would have 15 children; but along with Caroline, tragically five of their children are buried in the Cutler family plot at Christ Church cemetery: Malcolm (1827), Robert (1828), Elizabeth (1830), Wallace (1831), and Archibald (1837). Caroline died in 1856, aged 64. Malcolm, Robert, Elizabeth, and Wallace died as infants.

Archibald was the eldest child in the family. He was the first person from Guysborough to become a medical doctor. He studied medicine at the University of Glasgow and graduated before he was 21. He returned to Guysborough and practiced medicine for six months, but died on March 9, 1837 at the age of 21 years, 6 months. Mrs. Cox, who wrote a memoir of the early years of Guysborough titled *As I Remember It*, says:

> he returned to Guysborough from his studies and practiced for
> six months or so, but died when he was only twenty-two (his
>
> gravestone says 21 years, 6 months). He was lame and never well.

Portrait of Rob Roy MacGregor. It is reported that Duncan McColl had a very similar life sized portrait in his home in Guysborough, in a room which was used for Masonic meetings.

Another son, Jeffrey, made his home in New Glasgow, and eventually became the mayor of that town. It is known that as an elderly gentleman he summered at least one year in Guysborough, and his daughters would visit other Guysborough families. Their daughter, Caroline, married the Rev. Peter MacGregor, who for a brief period of time was the minister at the short-lived Presbyterian church in Guysborough. He was the son of Rev. James MacGregor of Pictou County, considered by many to be a leader amongst the Scottish Presbyterian settlers of that area.

Their daughter Caroline married the Rev. Peter Mac Gregor who for brief period was the minister at the short lived Presbyterian church in Guysborough. He was the son of Rev. James MacGregor of Pictou County, considered by many to be a leader amongst the Scottish Presbyterian settlers of the area.

Dr. Charles Rupert Metzler 1837 - 1870

by Mark Haynes

Born in 1837 in Truro, Nova Scotia, Charles Metzler attended Bellevue Hospital Medical College in New York State where he graduated as a Medical Doctor in 1864 at the age of 27. On his return to Truro, he learned of the need for an MD in Guysborough and moved there in 1865. Besides his regular practice he became a surgeon with the rank of Lieutenant in the Second Battalion of the Guysborough County militia in 1866. The Chedabucto Greys, as the battalion were called then, was formed in this year. On August 2, 1866, Dr. Metzler was also appointed Health Officer for the ports of Canso and Wilmot Township in Guysborough County.

On December 3, 1865, he married Harriet Louisa Wylde, the daughter of William Wylde, merchant, MLA and later inspector of fisheries for Nova Scotia. They went on to have three children; Harriet Elizabeth born on Sept. 19, 1866, Rupert H. in 1869 and Brenton Jarvis on June 14, 1870. In December of 1870 Charles came down with consumption. On the evening of December 13, Dr. Buckley, who became a practitioner in Guysborough in 1867, was called to his residence where he declared him dead at the age of 33. He charged his widow 50 cents for his services. Dr. Metzler was laid to rest in Christ Church cemetery on December 16, 1870. Mrs. Harriet Metzler went on to live until Aug. 29, 1888 when she died at the age of 57. The census of 1871 lists Dr. Metzler (deceased) as being of German decent while his wife is listed as being of English origin.

Dr. Metzler with two sisters, circa 1865. (NS Archives photo)

Christian Muller (Miller) 1751-1841

by Chris Cook

Christian Muller (Miller) was born in Germany in 1751, where he served as a soldier and attained the rank of Sergeant Major. In the mid 1770's, Britain fought wars in both the soon to be United States and In Europe. As a result manpower was getting short. Therefore German and Swiss colonists were called upon to form a regiment, as they had made an alliance with England. In 1775, the British government contracted with the Hanoverian army to raise up to 4,000 men throughout Germany, for service in the British infantry regiments, such as the 60th Regiment which later contained many of the first settlers of Guysborough. Christian Muller was a member of the 60th, and upon being settled in Guysborough, he received 250 acres of land granted to him on South side of Chedabucto Bay. He soon sold it and moved into the village of Guysborough. Much of the land of the 60th stretched as far as Fox Island from approximately Salmon River. Muller married Nancy Francheville (1764-1846) in Halifax, while awaiting transport to his land grant in 1784. They would be wed for 57 years.

The historian A.C. Jost recounts a story of Mr. Muller, " being on board a vessel travelling to Halifax to gather supplies. Upon the return, the crew had other plans, as Muller was forced off the ship and left on an island somewhere in the Jeddore area. The mutineers were eventually caught, taken to St. George Island, and hanged".

Muller became a prominent member of the new community of Guysborough. He held the office of Sheriff for Sydney County (Guysborough and Antigonish). On at least two occasions, Muller was required in his position of Sheriff, to give evidence regarding the outcome of a general election. In 1801, he was summoned to testify as to the result of the 1800 election since the ballots were lost. Later in 1815, the election of John Cunningham was contested. Muller was again required to give testimony as to the outcome. In 1819 he was one of the first directors of the Guysborough and Manchester Farmers' Society. Muller also kept an inn located at the head of the cove which still bears his name. On August 3, 1831, Muller hosted one of the greatest political leaders in Canadian history, "the reformer" Joseph Howe.

Howe, was on a province-wide tour to gain knowledge of the people and promote his newspaper, *The Novascotian*. He writes in some detail about his night spent at Muller's Inn. He paints a picture of a colourful and entertaining host:

> *...we enter the village of Guysborough, shrouded in mist and smothered in showers; and, by the advice of a fellow wanderer, betakes us to the most respectable public, over which Squire Christian Miller presides, and to which we would, in all seriousness, recommend those who are curious in the details of the Seven Years' War, or are insufficiently acquainted with the merits of Frederick the Great.*

Howe, goes on to describe that after travelling hours in the rain, they were weary and drenched. He relates that Mrs. Muller was very kind and accommodating to them, helping them gain comfort and rest. He continued to describe his evening and interaction with Christian Muller,

> *...that stretching ourselves in a large armchair in front of a blazing fire, we fell fast asleep,...when we were roused to behold our gallant host, charging by the side of the mighty Frederick the Great at the battle of Praque, and to listen to such an account of the whole campaign as we are satisfied is not stored up in any other head in the Province of Nova Scotia.*

Frederick the Great, leading the troops at the Battle of Prague, 1757. Christian Muller was present during the encounter. (www.internationalhistory.wodspress.com)

William Nixon 1749 – 1804

By Chris Cook and Mark Haynes

The first reference to William Nixon is on 7 June, 1774, when he married Ann James in Christ Church, Philadelphia. He obviously was a Loyalist for he ended up in Halifax following the Revolutionary War. A. C. Jost speculates he moved to Guysborough from Halifax to expand his business; likely realizing the potential for significant development in the early years of the settlement. After lands were relinquished or "abandoned" by those grantees who either didn't come to Guysborough or left soon after arriving, Nixon received a grant of 950 acres of land on July 3, 1788 and then on July 13 of the same year, he received a personal grant of 150 acres.

The historian H. C. Hart writes that Nixon's wharf and stores (storage buildings) were a little "north of the old fort, and his dwelling not far away." The fort referred to is Fort St. Louis, built during the French period at what is known today as Fort Point at the entrance to Guysborough Harbour. His buildings would have been along the presently named "Lower Water Street." Harriet Hart goes on to state that he built the first vessels in the new settlement at Ehler's Brook on the "Riverside." Today Ehler's Brook is called Fraser's Brook which flows into the Milford Haven River where the Havendale and Lesterdale signs are located on the Antigonish Guysborough Road. This is where the French built boats for the people in Louisbourg. A water powered mill existed here at this time. It is suspected Mr. Nixon took over and repaired the old mill to build his ships. He was said to have employed many men and vessels in trading.

One of the more interesting references to Mr. Nixon concerns an event in 1788 when about three-hundred Mi' kmaq came down from Cape Breton and landed their canoes on the long sandy spit which forms a breakwater to Guysborough Harbour. After a consultation, they drew their canoes across the spit and into the harbour where they immediately paddled over to Nixon's store. There they demanded flour, tobacco, molasses and rum which Mr. Nixon had to give them in fear of his life.

They then proceeded across the harbour to McColl's Island, where Captain Joseph Hadley had a house, and lit a large bonfire and feasted for three days. During this time Messieurs Cook and Hadley crept cautiously near and learned, through their knowledge of the Mi' kmaq language, that they planned to attack the main settlement of Guysborough once reinforcements arrived. This information was passed along and defences quietly built in preparation. In the meantime a priest from Cape Breton arrived and talked the natives into abandoning their plan and going back to where they came from.

William Nixon was one of three men (John Stuart and Thomas Cutler) who were ordered by Lieutenant Governor Sir John Wentworth in 1796, to distribute supplies to the local Native people. This required Nixon, Stuart, and Cutler to "buy and distribute... 200 bushels potatoes and 20 barrels herring." Lieut. Gov. Wentworth also sent Nixon 50 lbs of gunpowder, 100 lbs shot, 100 lbs lead, 200 flints, 100 yards baize, 20 blankets, 20 shirts, 20 coats, 20 trousers, 20 jackets, 20 yards blue cloth, and 20 barrels of flour, "all which I beg you to distribute among the Indians" and they are "to be faithful to the King, and to take arms with us in case of an invasion." By this date Mr. Nixon had attained the rank of Major in the Guysborough Militia.

William Nixon died on 30 March, 1804 at the age of 55. His burial is a bit of a historic mystery in that its method is no longer practiced. Hart records that he was "buried beneath his pew," as a mark of distinction. Likewise Rev. De La Roche and his wife were buried under the chancel of the church. Similarly, historic St. Paul's Church in Halifax has a burial crypt. Christ Church must have been built higher allowing for a crypt. This is supported by Judge Marshall's eye-witness account that the first church blew over in 1811.

William and his wife Ann had at least six children: William Jr (1778), Elizabeth (1782), Ann (1787), Maria (1790), Elizabeth (1794), and Mary (1774?). William and Ann died very young. William Jr. drowned in 1789 at the age of 11. Ann and Elizabeth died aged six and one respectively, five days apart in May of 1793. The original records of the cemetery state they died "both of a Quinsy." Quinsy is defined as an abscess in the connective tissue around a tonsil usually resulting from bacterial infection and often accompanied by fever, pain, and swelling. They are buried in Christ Church Cemetery along with their parents, William and Ann Nixon. His daughter Mary went on to marry first a Patterson and second Dr. Henry Inch.

Patrick Patton 1752 – 1816

by John N. Grant

Patrick Patton: Sergeant, School Master; b. 1752, d. 29 June 1816. He married Margaret Brown (d. 19 February 1833), and they had: Mary, (b. 30 May 1790); James Key, (b. 24 September 1791, d. 14 November 1791); David, (b. 17 November 1792, d. December 1792); Margaret, (b. 3 March 1794).

Guysborough was born of war. The American Revolution (1776-1783) split the old British Empire and many of those who had supported King and Country were forced to leave the new United States. On 16 May 1784, the first of the Loyalists arrived at Chedabucto and the process of settlement began. After the surveyors finished their work, homes, businesses, wharfs, and public buildings were built. Soon thereafter the leaders of the community turned their attention to education.

The first schooling was no doubt within family units, conducted either by parents or by private tutors hired by individuals or by groups of parents for their children. Others sent their children to relatives or friends who lived in areas where schools were already established. Itinerant school teachers and local private schools also provided educational fundamentals to some local children.

The first person identified as an established school master in the county was Patrick Patton of Guysborough. Patton, a sergeant in the 71st Regiment, arrived with the Associated Departments of the Army and Navy and received a grant of land. He married Margaret Brown at Christ Church in Guysborough and his children were baptized and, in some cases, buried there.

It is not clear if Patton ever occupied his rural lands or if he, disinclined to farming, became a teacher by force or by choice. Based on the 1811 claim that he had then twenty-five years of teaching experience, he may well have opened a school shortly after his arrival in Guysborough. However, about 1792, his position as a school master was solidified, as he was "employed and appointed as such by the Society from home" with a subsidy of £10 sterling paid by the Society for the Propagation of the Gospel.

The S.P.G. (established 1701) was a British philanthropic organization which acted as a missionary arm of the Church of England. Its mission was to support clergy and teachers throughout the British Empire. On 11 May 1786, the Court of General Sessions, the local government in Sydney (Guysborough) County asked the S.P.G to renew its missionary activities in the county. While there may have been concern in non-Anglican households about the religious message of a S.P.G school master "in the absence of any other, some parents risked 'doctrinal infection' and sent their children to these schools." Neither the church nor the state seemed overly concerned with the academic qualifications of the early teachers. The church demanded doctrinal soundness and the state 'sane conservatism' as the philosophical position of their schools. Patrick Patton no doubt fulfilled at least their minimum requirements.

The provincial government, however, became increasingly aware that it had a responsibility to promote schooling. The School Act of 1811 provided communities with financial support for local public schools and Guysborough moved quickly to take advantage of the opportunity. On 4 November 1811, Patrick Patton, with twenty-five years of teaching experience and who was judged by the local Schools Trustees as "a Man capable & fit for such an appointment – of Sober morals and steady conduct" was appointed School Master. It was Patton who, as Master, maintained regular school hours during the Gale of 1811 although "when the hour for dismission [sic] came the children had to crawl home, as none was able to stand before the fury of the tempest."

The location of the Patton's schoolhouse is known to us today. From research done through the former Guysborough Registry of Deeds, the "Guysborough School House Lot" was referenced in an 1835 transaction from Guysborough Merchant Isaac Wylde to the Methodist Church. This lot was located between the corner of Church St and Queen Street and the Corner of Church St. and Pleasant Street on the southern side of Church St. H. C. Hart in her *History of the County of Guysborough* states "Miss Charlotte Newton organized the first Sunday School in Guysborough in the old schoolhouse on the upper street in 1822."

The provincial government's support of schooling was based on the belief that it was "highly advantageous to the Youth of this Province to afford them easy means of acquiring useful knowledge in those essential parts of general Education which are necessary to persons of every rank and station in civilized Society … ." Useful knowledge was defined as reading, writing, arithmetic, and orthography (spelling) and these subjects comprised the basic curriculum of the Common Schools of the province. This was the curriculum that Patrick Patton was responsible to teach in his school at Guysborough. Pupils who wished to study more advanced work, before a local grammar school or academy was available, would have to make separate arrangements.

Whatever the other vicissitudes of his life, Patrick Patton continued to teach. By 1814 (?) he may have had a new school building at his disposal as the Court of General Sessions testified that year that "a School House has been Actually Built at Guysborough and Patrick Patton a School Master duly Licensed and appointed thereto, and that the sum of Fifty Pounds has been actually raised for the support of said School ... ."

There were no pension plans or expectation of retirement for most workers in 19th century Nova Scotia and Patrick Patton, based on the warrants for salary drawn in his name, taught for the rest of his life. He finished his term on 29 June 1816 and was buried with his children in Christ Church Cemetery. Nothing has been left that describes his ability as a teacher or his character as a man except his loyalty to his King and to his school.

After the passing of Patrick, Margaret lived for another 17 years; however evidence suggests she became quite impoverished. Research indicates that in 1825, the local Overseers of the Poor seized their home (located on the corner of Queen and Main street in Guysborough). Unfortunately for the Pattons, their twin infants (James and David) who were less than 2 months old, contracted the whooping cough in the late fall of 1792 and died within a month of each other.

The Patrick Patton house circa 1800, corner of Queen and Main St., Guysborough.

Godfrey Peart and family

By Chris Cook and Jamie Grant

Peart is the most frequently found name in the Christ Church Cemetery records. They are such a numerous clan that it was claimed half of the congregation of the Cook's Cove Methodist church was comprised of Pearts.

The family has a very long association with the area. The earliest record dates to 1764 when Thomas Peart, a resident of Canso, was involved in a court case there. In the family's lore he had been a privateer during the Seven Years War who had returned to fishing after the truce. The first Peart in the Guysborough records was Godfrey, who almost certainly was Thomas's son. He received a land grant at Cook's cove in 1787 along with eight others, most of whom had resided there since 1765. His grant was double that of the others and was likely meant to be shared with his brother John who, though not named, is known to have been present there.

Most of this group of nine were New England born fishing families who had come to the Liverpool area about 1759 and resettled here shortly after the Acadians left for Ste. Pierre et Miquelon in 1764. At least some of them had been fishing seasonally in Nova Scotia for many years; their acknowledged leader Joseph Hadley, for example, had a brother who drowned in 1737 returning to Massachuset from Canso. They were a very closely connected group, inter marriages being common. Godfrey Peart married Sarah Godfrey (nee Hadley) and from this union all the Pearts of Guysborough descend.

In Lois Wake Thurston's study of these families, she discusses the will of Godfrey Peart. She writes:

Godfrey Peart . . signed his will April 8, 1831, and the inventory was taken 12 Feb. 1834. He bequeathed to his wife Sarah his entire estate; (sic) after her death half the personal estate was to be divided into five parts between 'eldest son' John Godfrey Peart, son Thomas Peart, Frances Hart, Ruth McKeough, and William Wooten. Godfrey Peart's real estate was to be divided between sons John and Thomas and their issue, in tail, with 75 acres going to 'grandson Godfrey Peart, son of Thomas Peart.' Separate bequests of animals were made to grandson John Godfrey Peart, to Mary Davis and to Patrick Bailey. Wooten had been brought up from his infancy and served his apprenticeship with Godfrey Peart.

Godfrey Peart died in 1831 and his wife Sarah in 1842, aged 88. Both are buried at Christ Church. Godfrey's younger brother, John, is also buried there, having died in 1804 aged 39. The cause of death was recorded as scarlet fever. Godfrey and Sarah had at least two children; John (1786 – 1856) and Thomas (1788-1868). Both are buried at Christ Church. John was married to Maria Nixon. Three of their children are buried at Christ Church: William (1810 aged 2); Harriet (1827) and a second Harriet (1837 aged 9). The Guysborough school records for 1833-34 list Mrs. John G. Peart teaching school in Cook's Cove and her seventeen year old daughter Maria teaching a class of ten white and eleven black children and four adult males during the winter term in Guysborough. This is note worthy for at the time, since teaching was still a male preserve, integrated schools were rare as was adult education.

Thomas was married to Mary Cribben. She is also interred at Christ Church Cemetery (1791 – 1869). They had 10 children. Their first son, Godfrey (1811 – 1883) and his wife Martha Scott (1811 – 1881) are both buried at Christ Church along with three of their children; William in 1837 at aged 6; Frances in 1859 at age 19; and Stewart at age 83 in 1936. Stewart Campbell Peart was a high liner fishing captain who fished out of Glouchester, Massachusetts, whose family lived on part of the original Godfrey Peart grant. Capt. Campbell retired after a long sea career. He was the last Peart and second last person buried in Christ Church cemetery.

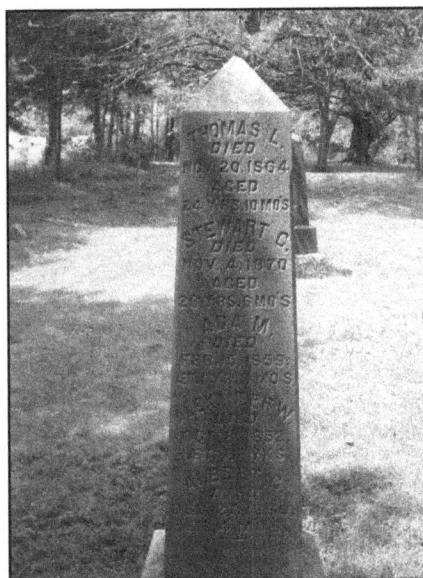

Children of T. C. and Frances Peart

T. C. Peart House, Main Street, Guysborough. Built circa 1843.

One son of Thomas and Mary, T.C. Peart, operated a store in the south end of the village, likely on the old Marshall location. It is clearly visible on the 1876 A.F. Church map of Guysborough County. T.C. Peart married Frances Scott in 1836. At least four of their children are buried at Church Church: Alexander (1852 aged 6 weeks); Ada (1859 aged 1); Thomas Jr. (1862 aged 22); Albert (1860 aged 4 months); and Stewart Campbell (1870 aged 28). For some time, T. C. Peart served as Guysborough's High Sheriff. The family was recorded by Mrs. Cox to have been living in a house at the southern end of main street in 1843 (see picture below). T.C. Peart is interred at Christ Church; having passed away in 1881 aged 67.

There are four other Pearts known to have been buried in the cemetery. Among them is an Esther Peart (1862 – 1889), but it is unclear where she fits in the family tree. There are also three others, but their first names are not legible in the cemetery records. There are as well many women who were born Pearts buried here but recorded under their married names. One of them was Henrietta Heinhaugh Martin, the mother-in-law of Dr. A. C. Jost.

Sarah Ringwood   1763 - 1831

by Mark Haynes

In all likelihood Sarah Ringwood was born in 1763 as Sarah Van Nostrant.[10] Her parents were Sam and Sarrah owned by enslaver C. Van Nostrant in Acquackeneck (now Passiac), New York (now New Jersey). He was

---

10

The first mention of Sarah Ringwood is in the list of free negro women arriving at Chedabucto in 1784 by author Harriet Hart, *History of Guysborough County*. In the 1785 Muster Roll for refugees receiving supplies from the British Government at Chedabucto, later named Guysborough, she is also listed. Author Carmelita Robertson of NS Museum Curatorial Report 91, *Black Loyalists of Nova Scotia: Tracing the History of Tracadie Loyalists 1776-1787,* points out her name is not in the Book of Negroes (BON) and assumes she must have originated from St. Augustine, Florida, for lists were not made of these black refugees. Unfortunately she did not think of the possibility Sarah Ringwood's name is not in the BON because she had a different last name then and acquired the name *Ringwood* sometime after 1783 (the date of the BON) and on or before 1784 (the date of the list in Harriet Hart's book). Christ Church records show she was 23 years old and already married when on July 30, 1786 she and her husband were baptized. This means she was around 20 years old in 1783, the year of the BON. A search of all unattached single females in the BON of either 19, 20 or 21 years of age reveals there is only one person named Sarah/Sally who fits that description and this is Sarah Van Nostrant, age 20 who was single and travelling with parents Sam and Sarrah Van Nostrant. It is highly likely this is the person who married Joseph Ringwood either at Port Mouton or soon after arriving at Chedabucto. The only other Sarah/Sally to have come here was a slave named Sally owned by Lieutenant Hudson who arrived in Country Harbour in 1784. If this is our Sally, she would be a runaway slave and would not be on the Muster Roll as only free negroes could get supplies. So this could not be her.

of Dutch origin who's ancestors heralded from the days of New Amsterdam
(now New York), when it was a Dutch colony. According to the Book of
Negroes, Sam, his wife and their daughter Sarah all ran away to the British
lines in 1777. Sam joined the Black Brigade of the British Army as a Loyalist
soldier. The family was stationed behind British lines until departing New York
for Nova Scotia in 1783 aboard the *L'Abondance*. After wintering in Port
Mouton, Sarah arrived at Chedabucto in 1784 but not her parents. It is not
known what happened to them. Perhaps they died in the miserable winter of
1783/84 or parted ways with their daughter and went elsewhere when she
met and married Joseph Ringwood (originally Wingwood). The exact date of
their marriage is not known other than it was in 1783 or 1784 when author
Harriet Hart lists her arriving at Chedabucto under the name Sally Ringwood.[11]

According to Anglican Church records both Joseph and Sarah were
baptized at Christ Church in Guysborough on July 30, 1786 as "Jospeh
Ringwood, 25" and "Sarah Ringwood, 23." In the 1785 Muster Roll, a list of
Loyalists who received supplies from the British Government, she is listed as
Sally Ringwood. While white Loyalists received land grants in 1785, black
Loyalists did not. Beginning in 1786 life began to get hard for early pioneers
when the British government stopped sending supplies. After the long winter,
life for settlers began to get even harder. So desperate was the situation that
William Wallbrecht built a boat at his own expense and sailed alone to Halifax
for supplies[12]. While this helped to offset the shortage of food for some white
settlers, it is doubtful if any of it was shared with the black Loyalists. Just how
desperate their situation was is discussed by historian Harriet Hart:

They (Negroes) suffered severely from famine and many died from want.
One poor man named Tom Thompson trying one very sever [winter] day to
go home from the lower part of town became so faint when passing Capt.
Ralph Cunningham's, that he thought he must ask there for help. As he
neared the door he heard a voice calling the dog, and fancying that the

[11] H.C. Hart, *History of the County of Guysborough,*
Mika Publishing Company, Belleville, ON, 1975, p 194

[12] Ibid p. 54.

inmates were taking that means of driving him away, he started again for Niggertown Hill, but he was so badly frozen he eventually lost his feet.[13]

This example probably explains the motive for theft by Sarah Ringwood which occurred on Oct. 10, 1787 when:

Sarah Ringwood, a Black Woman, brought before the Court for stealing a quantity of salt and French butter from Elias Cook . . . to receive thirty-nine stripes on her naked back at the Public Whipping post in Manchester."[14]

Thirty-nine lashes was a standard punishment at the time for theft because Jesus was struck thirty-nine times. Due to the plight of the black Loyalists, a leader arose amongst them by the name of Thomas Brownspriggs. He petitioned the Nova Scotia government for the grant of land promised to his people before they left New York. Finally in 1788 three thousand acres of Crown Land was surveyed at Tracadie and granted to seventy-four people. This worked out to be 70 ½ acres per person vs. the 5 acres of worthless land other blacks got just outside of Guysborough at what is known today as Sunnyville. Included in the Tracadie grant were Joseph and Sally Ringwood.[15]

Being baptized in Christ Church, Sarah/Sally made sure her children were also baptized there. As there was no church in Tracadie until 1827, each time she had a child, unless they owned a horse which was unlikely due to there being so few horses in the early years of Guysborough, she and her husband walked overland from Tracadie to have their children baptized. The church records state; "Sally, daughter of Joseph and Sally Ringwood, b. 25 July 1799/ Eva & Rosa, daughters of Joseph and Sally Ringwood, b. 23 July 1803."

---

[13] Harriet Hart, *A History of the County of Guysborough,* Guys. Hist. Soc., 2016, p. 54

[14] RG 34-311, NSA

[15] Brownspriggs Grant, Carmelita Robertson of NS Museum Curatorial Report 91, *Black Loyalists of Nova Scotia: Tracing the History of Tracadie Loyalists 1776-1787,* P. 116.

So in total it is known with certainty they had at least three children. Nothing else is known about Sarah/Sally Ringwood until she died and was buried in Christ Church Cemetery on January 14, 1831.

Samuel R. Russell   1806 - 1875

by John N. Grant

For forty years in the mid-1800s, no person in Guysborough County was more intimately involved with schooling than Samuel Russell. And it began by accident. In 1832, Samuel R. Russell, then 26 years old, left his home in Welton, County Northampton, England and boarded the Brig *Sir George Murray* bound for Quebec. After a safe voyage across the North Atlantic the ship was partially wrecked in the Chedabucto Bay and limped into Arichat, Cape Breton to discharge cargo and make repairs. Some of the passengers, including Russell, apparently decided to disembark there. Little is known of his life before he came to Guysborough or if he had earlier experience as a teacher. Nonetheless, Russell made his way to Guysborough, obtained a Common School teachers license and spent the next two years teaching at Guysborough Intervale where a school had been established by 1820 and a schoolhouse built by 1830. In 1834 Russell's school at the Intervale had fifty-five students and he earned a salary of £40. Some part of this was no doubt paid 'in-kind' including Russell's "Boarding, Lodging, and Washing" valued at "Seven Shillings per week." The arrangement was, at least, acceptable as it was noted that "the people have fulfilled their engagement with the Teacher and the Trustees are Satisfied with his conduct in the School."

In 1832, the Guysborough town schools trustees took advantage of the provincial legislation of that year which "provided for the establishment of a number of combined common and grammar schools in the province." In 1834 Russell was apparently convinced by Robert Hartshorne of Guysborough, a member of the Board of School Commissioners, to move to one of the schools "in the vicinity of Guysborough Town, and taught there for six months... ." In 1835, at the request of the School Trustees, Samuel Russell was "licensed to teach the Guysborough School, No. One." The curriculum of the Combined Common and Grammar School included the regular Common School courses as well as advanced instruction in "the classics, land surveying, navigation, and in the other practical branches of the mathematics." Under the circumstances Russell no doubt seized the opportunity presented to him and, except for a three and a half year return to the Guysborough Intervale School, there he stayed until 1864 when he was appointed Inspector of Schools for Guysborough County.

By 1840 the school had grown. The Commissioners reported that it "now averages from forty to fifty Scholars several of whom are studying Navigation and Surveying [,] others the Classics, Mathematics and Geography." The teaching staff had increased to match the demand for instruction. Russell was teaching geometry, algebra, geography, and English grammar and his co-worker the classics, geography, etc.

In the early 1840s, Samuel Russell was involved in another level of educational effort. The first Mechanics' Institute had been opened in Glasgow, Scotland in 1823. "There adult education had received its first impetus from the Industrial Revolution 'in the desire of mechanics for general scientific knowledge, and the willingness of the more intelligent part of the middle class to help supply the demand.'" By 1831 the movement had appeared in Halifax where both an Institute and a Mechanics' Library Association were introduced. The effort "to improve the minds of the rising generation" spread across the province and on 3 January 1843 the Guysborough Mechanics' Institute held its first meeting with Dr. Edward Carritt as president and E. I. Cunningham as the secretary. The Institute had already procured "an electrical machine and chemical apparatus" and the clergy, the medical doctor, and both of the local male school teachers were included on the list of speakers with Samuel Russell presenting lectures on mechanics.

Yet another of the educational impulses of the 1840s was the establishment of the first Guysborough Academy. The Academy was to be the apex of the public school system, attracting pupils who had succeeded in the Common and Grammar schools. It was active by 1843, combining the highest level of instruction with that of the Common and Grammar Schools in one building. The combined school had 72 scholars in 1846, (46 boys and 26 girls), ranging from seven to thirty years of age. Created and financially supported under the 1841 Education Act, the county academy's "primary purpose was the higher education of youth who in turn might supply the demand for teachers in the common schools." Samuel Russell was an important part of the new institution at the Grammar School level. However, the Academy was short lived and on 11 May 1849 there was a request to pay Samuel R. Russell "for teaching a Grammar School in the Town of Guysborough for 3¼ months ending 30 April last, the said sum being part of the Grant of £100 for the support of an Academy in the County of Guysborough, there having been no Academy taught in the said County since the commencement of the present year." It would be twenty years before a new Guysborough Academy was created.

In 1861, when Samuel Russell, as a long serving teacher, petitioned the House of Assembly for a one hundred acre grant of land, he referred to "several persons now in credible positions in Halifax" who "received their education" under his tutelage and asserted that his "success as a teacher has been as great as that of any in this County." The land grant from the province was meant to financially assist ageing teachers and Russell had been in harness almost thirty years. To support a family on a teacher's salary was difficult. Most teachers had to augment their income by out-of-school employment as subsistence farmers or by other means. Samuel Russell faced the same problem. He, in order to sustain his family of five sons and four daughters, "had been compelled whenever opportunity occurred to spend his hours out of school time in Surveying, Drafting, Writing or whatever might contribute towards the support of his family and without which the salary derived from teaching alone could not possibly have sufficed." Later in life, Russell also held various civic offices including Clerk to the Board of School Commissioners as well as Clerk of the Peace, and Registrar of Probate. "His taste for mathematical and meteorological studies led to his being chosen to prepare reports of the weather for this vicinity, which were regularly forwarded to Halifax and found to be very reliable."

One of the changes created by the Free School Acts of the 1860s was the creation of the office of Inspector of Schools in each county. In Guysborough County, the Rev. Joseph W. Forsythe, A.B., (Trinity College, Dublin), was appointed the first Inspector of Schools but by 24 August 1864 he had resigned. In his place the Board of Commissioners recommended Samuel R. Russell as his successor. Instead of thinking of slowing down, Russell entered a whole new phase of his life in education in Nova Scotia.

Russell's appointment was 'gazetted' (i.e. published in the Royal Gazette) on 14 September and by October he was busy "revising and locating" school sections, visiting schools, holding meetings, and serving on the Board of

Examiners to classify teachers in both the District of Guysborough and the District of St. Mary's. Russell was displeased with the condition of the school buildings throughout Guysborough County. He found "no school house near to the recommendations of the Council as respects size, site or accommodation" in the District of Guysborough although in St. Mary's there were seven schools that "though deficient in many respects," were superior to those in Guysborough. In his Inspectorate, like the rest of the province, "of the other houses reported, some hundreds are private property; other hundreds can scarcely be designated school houses, many being without floors, without glass windows, without plastering, without desks, without seats except rough slabs, without apparatus, or, if any, the scantiest."

There were plans in several communities for new school houses. Among the new school buildings, at least in the planning stage in 1865, was the new Guysborough Academy. Located in the shire town of the District, it was designed to serve as the finishing school for the students of the entire County. One of Russell's early concerns had been to improve the school buildings in Guysborough where he had first-hand experience and found them wanting. The solution came when the province's "grant to County Academies was restricted to County Towns" and Guysborough "formally accepted the offer" and, in 1863, was "already actively engaged in preparing the necessary building."

The Academy "contained two rooms in a lower story, with a larger room above. Its exterior featured an elaborate architectural treatment, more in keeping with that of contemporary urban schools; apart from the dimensions of the rooms, this structure did not adhere to the standard plans issued for academy buildings in 1864." Inspector Russell reported in 1866 that the "Guysborough Academy, measuring 75 by 33 feet, with sixteen foot posts, and a playground of one acre, is now not only finished and supplied with all necessary outbuildings, but furnished in all three departments with patent desks and seats, and is at this time in full operation with a staff of two male and one female teachers, and an attendance of at least 150 pupils... ." The following year he wrote that the Academy had attracted students from elsewhere in the county and one from Cape Breton, and concluded that the "Trustees and people of this Section deserve much credit for the building they have erected and furnished. The play-ground, embracing an area of one acre, is now surrounded by a neat fence, well painted."

The original Guysborough Academy built in 1865, centre of the picture on the crest of the hill with copula.

The job as Inspector of Schools was very demanding, requiring constant travel to the schools in summer and winter, by horse, by boat, and on foot. Meetings to deal with every conceivable issue were held and the Inspector had to attend. In his report of the school year ending 31 October 1871, Russell commented that "the very delicate state of my health made it impossible to visit many of the sections, but I did all I could... ." In 1871, Samuel and Isabella Russell still had five children living at home, ranging in age from 14 year-old George to 23 year-old Abigail. Two of their sons, John (21) and James (19) were employed as 'Clerks' but school inspectors were not well paid. However, due to his health, Russell retired from the Inspectorate in 1872, and in August he was replaced by William Hartshorne. Russell's retirement was not, however, the end of his involvement with schooling. By 12 November 1872

Russell was a member of the Board of School Commissioners and a year later was elected as Chairman. While the chairmanship was a one year term, Russell remained in office until May 1875, when the Commission minutes record that Chairman Russell "was too ill to attend the Board."

When Russell died in Guysborough in 1875 he was remembered as a man and teacher of ability. The Provincial Superintendent of Education, Alexander Forrester, had been impressed with Russell's Grammar School and Russell was recalled by succeeding generations as "an uncommonly expert mathematician." While it is argued that a teacher's influence can be enduring, in the case of teacher Samuel Russell and student Lawrence Hartshorne ,its impact was likely more direct. At 18 years of age Hartshorne was already a deep-water sailor having shipped out of Guysborough right out of school. He was sailing west from England when yellow fever broke out on his ship and both the captain and first-mate died, as did a number of the crew. Perhaps because of his schoolboy studies in navigation or other of the "practical branches of mathematics," Lawrence Hartshorne "brought the ship in safely. In recognition of his exploit [he] was given a first officer's ticket without examination." His success was, at least in part, attributed to the "good foundation" he received from Mr. Russell.

This might have been in Russell's thoughts when he wrote the last lines of his final report as inspector of schools in 1871. There he informed the Superintendent of Education "I hear continually, complaints from young men who wish to attend school in winter for the purpose of learning navigation, that they have no teacher who can teach them. I hope something can be done to afford our young men on the shores something better than second or third class teachers, as their business is on the sea, the country cannot do without them and they should, as far as possible, be educated for their occupation."

Perhaps Russell was ahead of his time with his concern about matching curriculum to the needs of the students. He was remembered well and went to his final resting place in Christ Church Cemetery confident that, in his own words; "I did all I could."

Donald/Daniel/David
Sellars/Sellers/Cellars

by Eric Emery

Donald Sellars was born approximately 1758 in either North Carolina or
Scotland. He died on the 13th of July 1848 in Guysborough County, Nova
Scotia. He married Margaret Keay in September 1797 in Guysborough
County. She was born in about 1776 in either New York or Scotland. She
died on the 28th of May 1848. She was the daughter of James Keay (1750-
1846) and Grizal [Nairn?] (1752-1846). Donald and Margaret had at least
11 children: Mary (1798-1872), Margaret (1800-1862), Donald Jr. (1803-
1881), Eleanor Jane (1804-?), Peter (1807-1807), Isabella (1814-?), James
(1815-1847), John Archibald (1816-1825), and Malcolm (1821-1900).

   The records consulted referred to him as Donald or Daniel Sellers
or Sellars. No records were found where he was named David Sellers. Since he
is listed on the Christ Church burial records as Donald Sellers, that is the name
that is used in the following biography.

   Donald Sellers, at the age of 77, was living at Guysborough
Intervale, Nova Scotia, and on the advice of his friends, applied for an
American Revolutionary War Pension. The year was 1836. In the application
he wrote that he joined the 6th Regiment of North Carolina at Wilmington,
North Carolina in the spring of 1776. He would have been 18 years of age at
the time. The 6th Regiment of North Carolina had been organized at Halifax,
NC. It had consisted of 8 companies of men from the Wilmington and
Hillsborough Districts. This area would have encompassed about half the State
of North Carolina and included all of the back country. The 6th Regiment of
North Carolina had been merged with the 1st Regiment of NC in 1778 and was
one of the Regiments in the North Carolina Brigade of the American
Continental Army.

The Pension Office rejected his claim for a pension even though some of the muster and pay rolls that had survived the war did list a Donald Sellers. However, other records showed Donald Sellers was dead. His heir had received a land grant for 640 acres in North Carolina in 1783 and his war pay vouchers had been paid to someone in 1785. The Pension Office wrote there had been a David Sellers in the army from North Carolina.

Donald Sellers had his youngest son, Malcolm, write a letter for him dated the 28th of March 1839. The letter was addressed to his Highness the President of the United States of America. In the letter he stated that he was the one and only Donald Sellers who had been in the 1st Regiment of North Carolina. Donald explained that the confusion over his name was due to the fact he could only speak Gaelic and the officers keeping the records could only speak English. He believed that was probably the reason why the officers had written David Sellers.

He then wrote, "And your Laws Say that if any parson [person] telling the Battles and ascertaining to them and the officers whom they Served under is Sufficient [to prove who they were]". In the letter he described the four battles he had been in and the various officers he had fought under during his time in the army. The final engagement he fought in had been at Charlestown, South Carolina in May of 1780. He had been wounded [he carried a musket ball in his leg the rest of his life] and captured by the British.

The information in the 1839 letter did not change the ruling of the Pension Board. They understood how the names Donald and Daniel could be confused but the names Daniel and David were much too different. Unless Donald could produce further proof of his identity they would not approve a pension.

Donald Sellers was a British prisoner of war in Charlestown from May 1780 until May 1781. At the time he was 22 years old, illiterate, and probably still spoke little English. The British decided that the best way to prevent the large number of prisoners which were escaping daily was to place them on prison ships moored in the Cooper river at Charlestown.

The prison ships were former transport ships used to carry the British army to Charlestown for the invasion and were no longer sea worthy. The masts were removed and all openings were boarded up. The prisoners were held below deck. The casualties from the filthy conditions were enormous. Many of the prisoners died from malaria, small pox, yellow fever, typhus, typhoid, and other fevers.

American prisoners on board a British prison ship (by John Trumbull, courtesy of Fordham University).

Donald Sellers in his 1839 letter wrote, "such a severe prison was more than what I was able to stand Being at the same time without Money and Clothes, eating up with lice and rotten with dirt [.] I laid down at night the same as I walked about all day neither Blankets nor anything But the hard boards to rest upon [.] And now if Congress had fulfilled their promise to me and had payed me my wages and Clothes as I was promised, then I would have been clothed as [a] Soldier and payed [paid] every Month."

In February of 1781 a solution to his situation of despair was offered in the appearance of Lord Charles Montagu, a former British Governor of South Carolina. The Governor of Jamaica, Major General John Dalling, needed troops for his dream of conquering the Spanish in Central America.

Lord Montagu was in Charlestown to find recruits from among the Continental prisoners for a regiment that he was to command for that purpose.

The recruiting notice read, "The prisoner may now gain his freedom, and those who had fortunes, and have lost them, may have an opportunity of acquiring new ones; whilst such who never possessed any may line their pockets with Spanish gold, by enlisting for three years in his Royal Highness the Duke of Cumberland's Regiment of American Rangers." The notice went on to offer, "immediate pay, proper clothing, enter upon free quarters, and receive a handsome bounty, upon their arrival in Jamaica." Also, Lord Montagu had promised they would not have to fight fellow Americans and that after the war they would be allowed to return to their homes or receive a land grant in Jamaica.

Donald Sellers had probably joined the North Carolina Regiment four years earlier mainly on the promise of pay, clothing and the advice of his friends. Now, once again on the advice of his friends, he decided to join a British Loyalist Regiment for the same reasons. In his letter of 1839, he justified his decision by stating that the Continental Congress had broken their promise to pay him his monthly wages and provide him with clothes. He had received nothing for three years. Since they had broken their promise to him, he felt no betrayal of honour by breaking his promise to them.

Montagu sailed from Charlestown in May 1781 with 500 former Continental prisoners. Donald Sellers' life of misery and almost certain death on board a prison ship was over.

He, along with other members of the Duke of Cumberland's Regiment, spent the next two and half years in Jamaica doing virtually nothing. Donald never saw another day of combat and he did not get rich on Spanish gold. On the last muster roll for the Regiment, taken in Jamaica when it was disbanded in August 1783, Donald Sellers name was listed in Lord Montagu's own Company. On this muster roll he was credited with three years service and he had indicated he was going to accompany Lord Montagu to Nova Scotia.

Lord Montagu knew his men could not return to the United States as they had been declared traitors. Using his political influence, he managed to convince the British government that his Regiment, even though consisting of former Continental soldiers, did qualify for free provisions and land grants in Nova Scotia. He would accompany his men to Nova Scotia in order to ensure they would be properly settled.

After a hazardous voyage from Jamaica, the first of two ships, each carrying 200 men, arrived in Halifax, NS in December 1783. Halifax was full of refugees and disbanded troops. Provisions and living quarters were in short supply. With Lord Montagu's connections, the Regiment spent the winter in the army barracks at Birch Cove, approximately five miles outside of Halifax.

Lord Montagu died in a cabin near his men on the 3rd of February, 1784. The men of the Regiment had lost their Benefactor. Many died and many others abandoned the Province before spring.

On the 16th of May 1784, what was left of the Regiment arrived at Chedabucto [Guysborough], Nova Scotia in order to receive their land grants. On the muster roll for the 20th of June, 1784 only 149 men were counted. Donald Sellers was listed as having no family and as a Private he was qualified to receive 100 acres of land.

The muster roll for Captain Gideon White's Company, dated the 25th of November 1784, contained Donald Sellers name. This muster roll noted these men had received their 120 days of provisions for the period from the 25th of November 1784 until the 24th of March 1785 at two thirds allowance.

Not much else is known about the conditions the men endured during the first few years at Guysborough, but in a letter dated in 1784, the privates in the Regiment had petitioned one of their former officers in England. In the letter they stated they wanted to become useful and industrious settlers in Nova Scotia but there were only ten women in the whole Regiment and few females in all of Nova Scotia. They asked for assistance from England in order to solve that problem.

In February 1785 Captain R.F. Brownrigg, the senior officer present, received the Duke of Cumberland's Regiment's land grant. Donald Sellers name was listed as receiving 100 acres of land. The Regimental land grant was located in three areas. Within each of these areas, the lots were divided into long narrow sections of land in order to ensure each man would get water frontage. This system, though fair to each man, was not practical for anyone who wanted to farm.

Donald Sellers got lucky when the lots were drawn from a hat. He drew lot 22, which was positioned in the centre of the 40 lots located on the Northeast side of Milford Haven River. It was a valuable lot to own. He also drew a town lot in 1790. It was useless to him except for the money he would receive when he sold it. From the land records it appears Donald Sellers sold lot 22 in 1787 and then started buying land at Guysborough Intervale. This area, formerly an early French Settlement, was approximately ten miles from the Town of Guysborough, at the head of Milford Haven River.

On the Provincial Assessment and Poll tax records, Donald Sellers name appears for the years 1792-1795. He was probably not a wealthy farmer as he was assessed at a rate of only one shilling. This was low compared to other settlers in the area.

Donald Sellers life changed for the better in September 1797. When he was 40 years old he had married Margaret Keay. She was 21 years old and the daughter of James Keay. The Nova Scotia Crown Land Map indicates that James Keay owned the lot next to his lot at Guysborough Intervale. Donald and Margaret Sellers settled down and raised at least 11 children on their farm over the next 50 years.

In the early years the only church in the area was the Anglican Christ Church, which was situated in the Town of Guysborough, nearly ten miles away. It was a good thing that the church had an afternoon service. On the first church assessment, in 1788, in order to support the church's clergyman, Donald Sellers had contributed three shillings. In 1796 when the first pews in the church were sold, he bought pew number 27. This pew was

123

one of the only 36 sold and even though it was off to the side and at the rear of the church, he still paid ten shillings for it. He also had to pay four shillings a year in rent. This would have been a lot of money for a poor farmer to pay. The church assessment of 1804 indicated that Donald Sellers was living in Guysborough Township. This strongly suggests that his house would have been on the south-west side of the river at Guysborough Intervale. When the pews were sold for the new church in 1814, Donald Sellers purchased pew number 39 for four pounds. Only 48 pews were sold. He continued to pay a yearly rent on this pew up until 1822, when pews number 39 and 40 were turned into a vestry room. Donald Sellers continued to be active in church affairs and in 1835 he contributed ten shillings toward a new roof for the church. In 1838, his son, Donald Sellers Junior rented pew number 16 and either Donald, or his son, continued to rent a pew in the church up until 1842.

Donald Sellers' name appears on the 1817 Census. He was listed as being over 50 years of age. It also listed: 1 son between the ages of 16 and 50 years old, 2 sons under 16 years of age, 2 women, and 3 girls. Of the 9 people in the family: 1 was listed as American born, 1 was listed as Scottish born, and the other 7 were listed as being born in Nova Scotia. It cannot be assumed that Donald was the Scottish born family member just because early in his life he only spoke Gaelic. There were many Gaelic speaking communities in the back country of North Carolina, especially after 1745. Both of Margaret's parents were born in Scotland. Margaret and her parents arrived in Nova Scotia from New York in 1783. She could have been born in either Scotland or New York.

On the 1838 Census, Donald Sellers was listed as a Farmer. Besides Donald there were 9 other members in his family: 3 males were over 14 years of age, 2 females were over 14 years of age, 1 female was under 14 years of age, and 2 males were under 14 years of age.

The Christ Church burial records showed that Margaret Sellers died on the 28th of May 1848 and was buried in the church cemetery on the 30th of May 1848. The burial records stated she was 72 years old. Donald died just over a month later on the 13th of July 1848. He was buried in the church cemetery on the 15th of July 1848. The burial records stated he was 90 years old. They had been married 50 years.

In conclusion, Donald Sellers' life can best be summed up by his son, Malcolm, who was still trying to obtain an American War Pension for his father in September 1846. Malcolm wrote that he was willing to do whatever the Pension Board required him to do, "so that his name [Donald], and character as a temporal Christian soldier, may go down to the grave in peace." The acknowledgment that Donald was telling the truth about his war record was more important than the money. Since Donald Sellers had been too poor to go himself to North Carolina to find former comrades who could verify his story, the person who collected his pay and received a land grant as his heir has remained a mystery. Donald Sellers never did receive a Pension.

Please contact the Guysborough Historical Society for a list of the sources used, more information on Donald Sellers, and a history of the Duke of Cumberland's Regiment.

Margery/May Shaw   1761 - 1828

by Mark Haynes

What is so interesting about the life of Margery Shaw is that it gives some insight into a successful Loyalist family farm. She and her husband Evan Shaw arrived in Guysborough in 1784 as part of the Association of the Departments. of the Army and Navy. They were given a land grant of 62 ½ acres at the Intervale, double the size of what a single person received because they were a married couple. It was excellent land due to it being flat and previously cleared during the French period. In addition to this country land they also got a town lot.

It is known they had a successful farm for they made the 1792 assessment roll for having more than six cattle. This put them in the top twenty-six wealthiest people in Guysborough. They were assessed an annual income of more than £5 for tax purposes. When Evan Shaw died in 1812, his will mentions his wife inherited half the cattle and half the sheep with their oldest son William inheriting the other half. The presence of sheep shows how the flat Intervale terrain was being used at this time. Just up the river towards Roman Valley was a cloth factory and a fulling mill testament to the volume of wool being produced in the area at this time. Both are visible on the 1876 Church map of Guysborough County.

All of Evan's farm land went to his son William. He was then instructed to sell off enough of his inherited assets to pay his brother James £40. He was to also give him a pair of oxen. So by 1812 they had raised a large flock of sheep and a herd of cattle including trained oxen. Neither his youngest son Alexander nor his daughters Isobel and Margaret are mentioned in the will. Shaw's Brook at the Guysborough Intervale still bares his name today. Margery Shaw died at the age of 67 in 1828 and was interred in Christ Church Cemetery along with her husband. She left all her possessions to her granddaughter Isabella Henderson except for two chairs and a table which went to her daughter Margaret Fraser. For this family the dream of coming to the new world and owning a successful farm came true, something that would never have happened had they returned to England.

Elizabeth Hopkins-Godfrey-Tobey 1720 – 1816

by Chris Cook

Due to the lack of records, the approximate twenty-year period between the exodus of the French from Guysborough in 1764 and the arrival of the Loyalists in 1784 is shrouded in mystery. Thankfully the south shore of Nova Scotia had well established communities and records for that era. The majority of the settlers starting to trickle into the Guysborough area came from Liverpool, N.S. during these two decades. Elizabeth Tobey could easily be considered the matriarch of both areas thanks in large part to her longevity, migrations, two marriages, and subsequent inter-marriages of many of her children, grand-children, and great grand-children across the 'nine old families' of Guysborough's pre-Loyalist period.

Elizabeth Tobey was born in 1720 in Chatham, Massachusetts to Elisha and Experience Hopkins. Her father, Elisha Hopkins, was a direct descendant of Stephen Hopkins, one of the Mayflower settlers almost 120 years prior. When she was 18, she married Benjamin Godfrey Sr., her second cousin. They would have at least two sons; Benjamin Jr (1740) and Gideon Godfrey. Sometime prior to 1756, Benjamin Sr. passed away and Elizabeth married Nathanial Tobey in 1756 at the age of 36 while still living in Chatham, Mass.

In 1762, Benjamin Jr. married Bethiah Atwood in Chatham. About this time fishermen were leaving the Cape Cod area for Nova Scotia's south shore, mainly to Liverpool. Among the group were Nathanial and Elizabeth Tobey, along with her sons Benjamin and Gideon Godfrey.

Nathanial and Elizabeth's time in Liverpool would be brief. Here they received a grant of land in 1764, and another later in Port Medway (1766). At this time, Capt. Joseph Hadley was established in a seasonal fishery in Guysborough, and was regularly commuting between Guysborough and Liverpool. He is known to have been closely associated with Nathaniel Tobey as Elizabeth's son, Gideon, was married to Capt Joseph's daughter. Therefore, her 'connections' made the removal from Liverpool to Guysborough palpable for Nathaniel.

About 1768, Capt. Joseph permanently settled in Guysborough. Elizabeth and Nathaniel, along with a collection of other families (Cook, Horton, Ingersoll, Godfrey, Peart), soon followed. A large tract of unoccupied land originally granted to Rev. Richard Byron, was available to settlers. Due to the conditions of the original grant not being met, the British government was anxious to fill this grant with colonists. Almost 20 years would pass before the families received permanent title to their properties upon which "they had built homes and made considerable improvements." About this period the wife of Elizabeth's son, Benjamin, passed away. It is unclear if he was in Guysborough then, but two of his daughters moved in to live with Elizabeth and Nathaniel.

Nathanial Tobey died approximately 1795. This was the second time in Elizabeth's life that she was left a widow; the first when she was 25-30 years of age and the second at approximately 75. She remained in Guysborough, likely residing with her son Samuel Tobey. She outlived her Godfrey children as Gideon passed about 1786 and Benjamin in 1807. When Elizabeth died in 1816 at the age of 95, she was survived by her two Tobey children (Samuel and Elizabeth Cook), 24 grandchildren, 66 great-grandchildren, and 12 great-great-grandchildren.

Information taken from "The American Genealogist" Vol 66, No., 1991. Elizabeth Hopkins Godfrey Tobey of Massachusetts and Nova Scotia: Her Identity and Her Children. Lois Ware Thurston.

Edmund Twiford   1774 - 1843

by Jamie Grant

This man's name doesn't appear on any of the known documents of his day, not on any census, land transfers or church records. Even his death is unrecorded. If not for his tombstone and for the following account written by Harriet Hart, who was a young girl when he died, he would have been completely forgotten.

Guysborough has had many residents in by-gone days, whose   names and characteristics should be preserved. A few of these are subjoined. One was 'the old gardener,' as he was familiarly termed. He had the oversight of many of the gardens about town. He delighted in large plots perfectly square, which he bordered with currant and gooseberry bushes alternately. His asparagus seemed always to come up in straight rows, like a company of soldiers. His tomatoes, which he called love apples, were only to be looked at with admiring, wondering eyes, to taste was forbidden, as he declared they were poisonous, and we were certain that on horticultural points he was infallible. His name was so little used that after his interment in the burial ground attached to Christ Church, just at the left of the entrance, the children tracing out the epitaph above his last resting place enquired, "Who was Edmund Twifordd"

All we could tell them is that he was born in Creiton, Devonshire, England and married Mary Miller in Halifax in 1808. It seems likely he was trained as a gardener in the formal style popular at that time in Europe. Tomatoes were then commonly called love apples and considered poisonous in England. But where he lived, when he came to Guysborough and who erected his tombstone are unknown.

Flower garden in back of the residence of W.H. Buckley, 1932.

Though there is no mention of Twiford by name, his influence on the village's landscape was commented on by Joseph Howe in his "Eastern Rambles". In 1831 he visited Antigonish, Sherbrooke and Guysborough. He was unimpressed with the first two but Guysborough delighted him with its natural beauty and its "beautiful gardens". Howe was taken with the "tasty arrangement and agreeable disposition" of the plots of vegetables and flowers. He also complimented the ladies on the quality of their current wine. The unsung Twiford's labours had born fruit and continued to do so for many years after his death. Gardening has remained a "favourite amusement" to the present day. The Guysborough Garden Club grows vegetables for the local food bank and maintains decorative shrubs and flowers in what Howe might well consider a tasty arrangement. Perhaps Edmund Twiford is secretly their muse.

The Unknown Soldier ? – 1796

by Christopher Cook and Jamie Grant

The Christ Church cemetery records have an unusual entry on October 19, 1796. It reads: "A soldier belonging to Fanning's Corps at the Island of St. John's...by the hosting of a blood infection" From the *Loyalist Connection* website the following information can be found about the Fanning Corps:

Edmund Fanning, the Colonel of the King's American Regiment in the American Revolution and from 1783-1786 Lieutenant Governor of Nova Scotia, was appointed Lieutenant Governor and Commander-in-Chief of the Island of St. John in 1786. In 1793, at the outbreak of war between France and England, he organized the local militia into three regiments: Queens County Regiment; Kings County Regiment; Prince County Regiment; and an independent volunteer company called the Loyal Independent Caledonia Company of Volunteers. Not content that the militia companies and the volunteer company could provide adequate defence for the colony, in the fall of 1793 Fanning requested the authority to raise a regiment similar to the volunteer corps raised in Nova Scotia and New Brunswick. In 1794, he was granted permission to raise and command the St. John's Island Volunteers, a corps of two hundred volunteers divided into two companies. The officers were to be appointed from regular half pay officers living on the Island, including many Loyalists, and the pay for the corps was to be the same as the pay in the regular army. When the name of St John's Island was changed to Prince Edward Island in 1799, Fanning's corps changed its title and became, His Majesty's Prince Edward Island Fencibles. In 1802, Great Britain and her enemies signed the Treaty of Amiens and the Regiment was disbanded.

Though the circumstances surrounding this soldier's death will never be known, it appears he died of a septicaemia, commonly known as blood poisoning. It is impossible to know how he became infected. It might have been a cut, a puncture wound or even a scratch. Many WWI soldiers died from small scratches or abrasions which became infected and until the development of antibiotics in the 1930's, there was no effective treatment. His was just one of millions of deaths that empathize how perilous life was before the development of modern medical science.

There is also no way to know what brought him to Guysborough, but the presence of three medical practitioners in the village seems a likely explanation. The regimental surgeons Dr. James Boggs and Dr. Paul MacPherson and Sgt. Ludevic Joppe, a surgeon's assistant who was always referred to as Dr. Joppe, were practicing in the area and perhaps the ailing soldier was brought to one of them for treatment. The symptoms of blood poisoning would have been all too familiar to doctors of the period.

All any of them could do was ease his pain, death was inevitable. He may or may not even have been alive when seen by a doctor. Why though wasn't his name recorded in the burial records? Perhaps his corpse was identified only by regimental insignia but just as likely Rev. J. W. Weeks didn't bother to ask. Some of the others he buried were identified as "aged black woman", "Anderson - very old", "Dinah" and "chile Mackay." Whoever he was, he was laid to rest in Christ Church Cemetery in an unmarked grave and unidentified in the church records.

It is hoped that some of the local veterans of the earlier American Revolutionary War provided suitable military honours to a fellow brother-in-arms who died in the service of the King.

William Wallbrecht 1747 – 1804

by Jamie Grant

It seems an injustice that so frustratingly little is known of the heroism of this dauntless man. He seems to have been single when he arrived at Chedabucto aboard the *Diana* in June of 1784. Since there were no Wallbrecht women or children on the muster roll and no marriage recorded later, he seems to have remained single for the rest of his life. His name suggests he may have been one of the six Hessians on board, but he could just as well have been one of the 51 men from the Civil Departments of the Army and Navy. He was granted 200 acres and lived close to the Upper Narrows of the Milford Haven. He must have prospered as a carpenter, since he was one of only 25 men on the Assessment Roll of 1792 (Guysborough and Manchester) who paid over the minimal amount of tax.

While the Loyalists fared reasonably well during the first two years, their lot got much harder after the British Government stopped sending provisions. The historian Mrs. Harriet Hart describes their plight: "In summer there was no lack of food, but when the long winter came, their want began, first with the poor and impoverished, and then among those who never refused to share their fast diminishing stores with their less-favoured neighbours." On one such occasion, the winter of either 1787 or 1788, Hart tells us that, "William Wallbrecht, who was an ingenious courageous man, lived at the Riverside, on what is now the Creshine farm. At one time he built a large boat and went alone in it to Halifax, and returned with a full cargo of provisions." This he shared with his neighbours.

Wallbrecht died in 1804 at the age of 57, leaving his entre estate to John Creshine's family (then spelled Greisheim), referring to John as his *good friend*. He left his "back lands" and carpenter's tools to thirteen year old John Creshine Jr. To their third son George, he left his mare and colt and to their oldest daughter Mary, he bequest his bed and bedding. He even thought of the younger girls with pieces of furniture or a number of sheep. Perhaps a shared German heritage cemented their friendship.

This forgotten hero of the earliest days of the Guysborough settlement is interred in an unmarked grave, in an unrecorded plot in Christ Church Cemetery; an unfitting fate for one who gave so much. How many lives did Wallbrecht save by that one remarkable feat of courage of sailing to Halifax for supplies?

Rev. Joshua Wingate Weeks 1738 – 1803
&
Sarah Weeks 1737 – 1817

by Chris Cook

We can be certain that Mrs. Sarah Weeks is buried in Christ Church Cemetery, her death occurring in 1817 and duly recorded in the church records. She was born Sarah Treadwell in Ipswich, Massachusetts and married Joshua Weeks in the early 1760's. They had eight children including Rev. Charles Weeks who followed in his father's footsteps to also become a rector of Christ Church. Sarah, like most married women of her day, does not appear in the local records other than that of her death. She likely focussed her efforts on the home front as wives were expected to do.

It is less clear where her husband's remains were laid to rest, there being no account of his death in the Christ Church records or in the records of any other Anglican church in the province. It seems almost certain however that he too was interred in Christ Church Cemetery. His death in 1803 occurred within the period of a gap in the known records (1798 - 1803). It seems likely they were somehow lost at some point during the more than two centuries since.

The issue is also complicated by both Rev. Weeks casual approach to record keeping. The records left by the both of them reflect a low level of interest in this aspect of their duties. Rev. Charles Weeks did not even record his own father's burial, and furthermore Rev. Joshua Weeks does not have a gravestone in the cemetery. Perhaps its poetic justice since the final resting place of so many of the earliest residents will never be known.

Rev. Joshua Weeks lead a colourful life. He fled for his wellbeing during the American Revolution as an ardent Loyalist and devout proponent of the King's Church. Accounts remain of his time in Marblehead, Mass. where, from the pulpit, he chastised a member of the congregation for rebelling against the British Crown and therefore, the Anglican Church. That member of the congregation was none other than George Washington. If nothing else, we can concur that Weeks lacked neither bravery nor conviction to take such a public stance.

Joshua Weeks went on to become a Rector at St. Paul's Church, Halifax, eventually finishing out his career and passing into relative obscurity in Guysborough in 1803. From the records available, including several early histories of the Anglican Church in Guysborough, all authors conclude there is no known location of Rev. Joshua's place of burial. By the process of elimination and the application of logic, Rev. Joshua must be buried in Guysborough though. H.C. Hart notes, that Sarah Weeks remained in the Rectory thirteen years after her husband's death, until she passed in 1817. Knowing she is buried in Guysborough, it is highly likely that Rev. Joshua is buried here also.

According to Arthur Eaton, in his 1891 book *The Church of England in Nova Scotia and the Tory Clergy of the Revolution,* Reverend Joshua Wingate Weeks was the eldest child of Colonel John and Mrs. Martha Weeks. He was born at Hampton, New York and graduated from Harvard College in 1758. He was ordained in England in 1761, and in 1762 became rector of St. Michael's Church, Marblehead, Massachusetts. In 1775, he was driven from that place by "the political commotions of the time," and took refuge with the Rev. Jacob Bailey, his brother-in-law, at Pownalboro, Me. He returned to Massachusetts however, and in 1778 asked permission to leave the country. His petition was rejected, but he left anyway. For a time he was in England, whence he came to Nova Scotia in 1779, three weeks after Mr. Bailey arrived.

The Reverend Thomas Wood died December 14, 1778 and Mr. Weeks was appointed missionary to Annapolis in his place. Instead of going there he remained in Halifax for a few months, and then sailed for New York. In November, 1779, Mrs. Weeks and their eight children came to Halifax, and there, in the spring of 1780, Mr. Weeks joined them. He seems to have preferred living in Halifax rather than going to his mission, and for a time was a garrison chaplain, and assistant to Dr. Breynton, the rector of St. Paul's. Dr. Mather Byles was in Halifax at this time, and was likewise a garrison chaplain. Dr. George Hill, the historian of St. Paul's Church, thinks that Dr. Byles may have been the senior chaplain with Mr. Weeks the junior chaplain. For a time Mr. Weeks drew from the Society of the Propagation of the Gospel seventy pounds a year, which was half the salary apportioned for the Annapolis mission. The Society, not pleased with his remaining away from his work, in 1780 appointed the Rev. Jacob Bailey to the mission. In 1785, the Rev. Dr.

Breynton went to England, and until his successor, Mr. Stanser, was inducted into the rector ship in 1791, and indeed somewhat longer, Mr. Weeks had either sole or partial charge of St. Paul's parish, Halifax. After that he officiated, it is said, at Preston and Guysborough, and "could have been settled at Digby." Like most of the other Loyalist clergy who came to Nova Scotia, he was poor, sometimes in actual distress; he died in Nova Scotia in 1803, and has still descendants in the province.

Many of Rev. Weeks' sermons still remain in the Nova Scotia Archives and Records Management of his time spent in Halifax from 1785 – 1791. Upon the death of the pioneer clergyman of Christ Church, Peter De La Roche, Rev. Weeks came to Guysborough and served out his remaining years of clerical duties in the village. According to Hart, Weeks' first record in Christ Church was Oct 4th, 1795. It is known from the local records, that Joshua and Sarah Weeks lived at the end of the Belmont peninsula (the location of the former Osprey Shores Golf Course). This area was appropriately named "Minister's Point" and still has this name today. Foundation-like depressions also remain at Minister's Point. Interestingly, the grandson of a prominent early church member, Thomas Cutler, named Nelson Ballaine, was known to have been buried at Minister's Point, as his gravestone was plowed out of the ground there in the early 20th century.

Years after Rev. Joshua's passing, Sarah Weeks at the age of 74, petitioned Sir George Prevost, Lieutenant Governor of Nova Scotia to acquire clear title of land that had been promised to her late husband; due to her destitute and impoverished state. It reads, in part:

That your petitioner's late husband on account of his loyalty to His Majesty, was obliged in the late Revolution in the United States of America to leave his property and his prospects at Marblehead where he was settled and joined His Majesty's forces. That about the Peace in 1783 he came to this Country to settle, and resided some years in Halifax. In 1796, he came to this place to reside and remained here as the Clergyman until his decease, which happened in the winter of 1803. Some time prior to his death, he obtained from Government a Warrant of Survey of 1000 acres of land, which was surveyed and located to him at or near Salmon River in this County, which was given him in part compensation for his losses, in the late American War. That in consequence of his having a large family of children to provide for and educate, he died without making proper provision for his widow, whereby she was left destitute of the means of taking care and maintaining herself. This 1000 acres of land and a few moveable effects was the whole that was left. It was the wish of the late Husband, as well as the whole of the children after his decease, that Your Petitioner should have a grant in her own name o this 1000 acres of land, which would have enabled her to maintain and support herself more comfortable, than otherwise she would and application was made by Your Petitioner to our late Lieutenant Governor Sir John Wentworth but upon his removal nothing was done in it. The little personal property left Your Petitioner is nearby all expended and she has been under the disagreeable necessity of applying to her children for assistance, which at the best precarious, and very unpleasant, although they are disposed to do all in their power to assist and help her upon these consideration. Your Petitioner is induced to hope Your Excellency will be pleased to give her a Grant of that 1000 acres...

Rev. Joshua and Sarah Weeks were excellent examples of Loyalists who become the pioneers of Eastern Canada in the 1780's. Being loyal to the British Crown and the Church of England, they were forced to face an unknown country due to their political and religious convictions. They eventually settled and became an integral part of a new community; perhaps leaving the strife and turmoil of the past behind them in the pioneer community of Guysborough.

Matthew Welsh ? - 1834

by John N. Grant

Welsh, Matthew, Military, Blacksmith, b. [?],d. April 1819; m. 1st:, [?], Ann, b. c. 1770, d. 2 June 1805, 2nd: 22 November 1806, Elizabeth Jones, b. [?], d. 1834; No Issue. Church of England.

Matthew (or Mathew) Welsh arrived in Guysborough with the Associated Departments of the Army and Navy in June 1784. It included representatives of the 71st and 72nd Regiments, Tarleton's Legion as well as various other military personnel that were described as a "heterogeneous grouping of persons who had little but their need in common." Like many of his fellows, Welsh received land on the wooded hills of the Milford Haven River. His grant was in the North East Division #4, Block R, front land, No 31, 30 acres and, in the Backland No E 3, 70 acres.

Welsh, however, was a skilled blacksmith, an important trade at that time, and he prospered. Welsh also farmed and, as the entries in the Registry of Deeds verify, did some dealing in the purchase and sale of land. In time his business grew to the point that he took apprentices into his shop; teaching them his trade in exchange for their services.

Matthew Welsh was an involved citizen. He acted as a surety in legal cases in the 1780s and served on the Grand Jury in both the 80s and 90s. In 1791, he was a member of the jury in the King vs Daniel Hays case, the first murder trial held in Guysborough.

Welsh was also an involved member of the Church of England, contributing to it both financially and by his service. He was a Vestry Man almost continually between 1798 and 1815 and was a regular contributor to the church's coffers. By October 1796, Welsh purchased pew #2 for £1:0:0 and paid an annual rent of 6 shillings until 1815. That year, Matthew Welsh, Gentleman, purchased pew #29 in the new Christ Church, after the first was destroyed by the Gale of 1811. Pew 29 cost £10:5:0 and also carried an annual rent of 10 shillings. After Welsh's death, his heirs continued to rent the pew until 1821.

Worshipful Brother Welsh was also an active member of Temple No 7 of the Masonic Lodge, (organized in January 1784), and served in various offices including as Master in 1796. His involvement in the religious and civic affairs of the community brought him into contact and friendship with the other leading men of the settlement.

In 1818 Matthew Welsh made a Will and by April 1819 he had died. By the provisions of his Will, Welsh made a generous contribution of £1,000 annually to the educational needs of the children of the community. After providing for his apprentices, brothers Michael and Thomas Murphy, and his wife Elizabeth, he explained that "having made what money and property I shall be possessed of since my arriving and settling in said Township and ... [wish]... to shew (sic) my gratitude to those from whom I have received the same by bequeathing ... [it]... to their offspring in the most useful manner I can devise...." He directed his Trustees, on the death of his wife, to sell his property at public auction and invest the proceeds. The interest that accrued was to be used to help "maintain a free Grammar or English School," or an Academy in Guysborough "for the benefit and advantage of the rising generation."

While it has been argued that the Welsh endowment was not handled to its best financial advantage, it has nonetheless served the community well. When the Guysborough Academy of the 1860s was built, part of the local funding came from the Matthew Welsh estate. The Trustees "loaned the Guysborough School No 1 the sum of $1,104.74 or the equivalent in old Nova Scotia currency of £285 with interest of 6% for 8 years."

Two hundred years later, the proceeds from this fund, which may be one of the first private endowments of public education in the province, are still being used as the enlightened blacksmith of Guysborough wished. Today, the Matthew Welsh legacy continues to benefit the "rising generation' by providing bursaries to financially support the students of Guysborough Academy.

Esther Whitman 1771 - 1814

by Mark Haynes

Very little is known of Esther Whitman, however she's included in this compilation of biographies as her life is so representative of countless pioneer women of the era. She was born on October 4, 1771 to parents William Atwater Sr. and Esther Turtle in Cheshire, New Haven, Connecticut. Her parents and their eight children fled to Guysborough in 1786 as Loyalists and settled in Manchester on lands acquired by her father as part of the Hallowell Grant. She married George Whitman, an acquaintance of her father, on March 13, 1788 at the age of 17 and settled into the life of a farmer's wife. Though it cannot be said with certainty it was an arranged marriage, it can be said it was a highly encouraged one. She had her first child the following year. While her husband became a successful farmer as evidenced by his becoming one of the members for Manchester in the Guysborough and Manchester Farmers' Society, she went on to have at least twelve children who were known to have survived. At the age of 42, three months after the birth of her last child, she died of heart failure on February 11, 1814 and was interred in Christ Church Cemetery. When her cause of death was discussed with a local present day doctor, it was her opinion she was simply worked to death. Her husband immediately married again the same year to the widow Margaret Irwin. They had another seven children for a grand total of nineteen offspring for Mr. Whitman.

Isaac Wylde   1790-1837

By: Chris Cook

Sometimes we don't always end up where we thought we would . The story of Isaac Wylde is one such example. Isaac was born at Oldham, Lancashire, England in 1790. As a boy, he dreamt of the 'New World' and became desirous for adventure and wanted to see America for himself. At the age of 21, he sailed from Liverpool, England, in September of 1811bound for Halifax. Near the Grand Banks of Newfoundland, the ship encountered a significant gale. He eventually arrived safely to Halifax, and there, two years later, married Lucretia Peck (who lived to be 99).

In 1817, he visited Guysborough, and was so impressed with the community that he decided to settle here permanently. He went on to partner with Duncan McColl in successfully procuring good teachers for the schools in the area. With other community leaders he was one of the founding members of the Guysborough and Manchester Farmers Society in 1819. Such societies cropped up across the Province and served as advocacy organizations to draw attention to farmers of the importance of their work and the need and means for its improvement. The local Society was given the responsibility to oversee the Reserve Lands of Manchester. Prizes were annually awarded for a sundry of produce and for the greatest land improvement. Inspectors were appointed to visit the various farms and send in reports to the Provincial organization (Central Agricultural Society). They also organized early exhibitions including cattle shows and ploughing competitions. Isaac also enjoyed military exercises, and at the time of his death in 1837, he was Lieutenant Colonel of the Second Battalion of the Guysborough Militia. (H.C. Hart, *History of the County of Guysborough).*

In the 1838 Census the "Widow Wylde" household consisted of one girl under the age of six, two boys and two girls between the ages of 6-13, and three males and three females, including herself over the age of 14. All accounts indicate Isaac and Lucretia had a 'large family' and the census indicates there could have been as many as 11 children over a 24 year marriage. Among them was William, a leading merchant of Mulgrave, an MLA for Guysborough County and Provincial fisheries inspector. Their daughter Elizabeth married Edward Irish Cunningham, a prominent local merchant who continued business on his father-in-law's site and was the mother of Guysborough historian Harriet Cunningham-Hart.

Isaac Wylde house, Guysborough, built circa 1832.

Thoughts on Old Cemeteries

by Jamie Grant

"... think of the bones, the crosses and stones of their fathers that came

there before them ... "   Stan Rogers

A century ago the *Canso Breeze* published an article by Duncan
Floyd which in abridged form appears as the forward of this book. In it he
speaks passionately of the debt his generation owes to the pioneers of the
community. He reflected on the courage, resolution and fortitude with which
those intrepid men and women faced the perils and privations of the
wilderness. Floyd expressed both sadness and anger that the many sacrifices
they endured for principle were so lightly regarded by those who followed.

It is not surprising these thoughts occurred to him while alone in a
pioneer burial ground, for old cemeteries have long been recognized as places
that elicit emotion and inspire thought.

Few visitors to old graveyards escape the feeling of melancholy.
Since all human life is precious, being surrounded by monuments to its loss
naturally saddens. Death is always sad, but doubly so when children die, as so
many children of the pioneers did. Their lives cut short, never having fully lived,
they are doubly dead. Sadness may morph into anger or pity or to more
positive emotions such as gratitude for the advantages we now enjoy, or to
wonder of the majesty of life, of which death is only a part.

The more contemplative may turn to another type of question,
such as, why would a loving God permit the deaths of so many children or
what part does pure chance play in our lives. The religious may seek answers in
theology and the secular in science while others concede that such questions
may be unanswerable. But, we are driven by our need to understand. Old
tranquil cemeteries are ideal places for thought where we can ponder away
from the demands and distractions of life.

Perhaps it was during one of his frequent visits to local graveyards
that Charles Bruce conceived his concept of a "community in time". He had a
deep-rooted attachment to the area but necessity had forced him to move to
central Canada where, like so many economic refugees, he pined for home. He

had lost his community in physical space but retained membership in a "community in time"; though living else where he and his descendants retained hereditary membership in this community.

So then, all descendants of those who once made their homes here are one with those of us who live here now, neighbours in time. It also follows that Christ Church, our pioneer cemetery, is a monument to our common past, a symbol uniting us in a "community in time".

A Review of the Records

by Chris Cook

A general idea of the conditions faced by our pioneers can be extrapolated from the biographies of individuals. All shared the same challenges, privations, fears, frustrations and hopes, so to some extent one's story is the story of all. However, period records such as those of Christ Church also provide valuable information of an objective nature from which statistics can be derived.

For Example, causes of death were quite well documented by the ministers of the day between 1787 and 1797. The records then vanish until 1804. Causes of death were given for many until 1834. The death entries then become just a list of vital statistics until 1865, without any supplemental information. Afterwards, any extra detail seems to be at the whim or practice of the particular priest or minister in charge. The following commentary will therefore discuss causes of death or any additional information provided.

First, there is statistical information available from the burial entries. For example, 22% of all known burials where those of children under the age of 16. This equates to 167 of the 764 known burials In Christ Church cemetery. Indeed, the first recorded interment was July 19, 1787, of an Ann Farfer, aged 16 days. Just three years later, her sister Mary, succumbed to small pox.

Becoming a healthy adult in the early 19th century was somewhat of an accomplishment; especially considering that medical care was primitive and sporadic, and at times provided by individuals of questionable credential. As well, there were many conditions for which there were no known cures. In just over a week between late January and early February of 1790, there were seven children who died of small pox. Between April and June of 1804 scarlet fever swept through the community which claimed the lives of seven children. Siblings Jane and Elizabeth Murphy were among those who fell victim.

Another common cause of death was dropsy. Dropsy is an old-fashioned term for general edema (the accumulation of fluid under the skin that causes significant swelling). Dropsy could occur in pregnant women, those with heart conditions or high blood pressure. It would have been a significantly painful and unpleasant leading to eventual death. Other causes of death listed in the records included: the common cold, whooping cough and quincy (an abscessed infected tonsil).

There were additional causes of death given that we'd seldom see with today's lifestyle and modern comforts. They are indicators, however, of the occupations and work conditions which many residents faced on a daily basis. There were four men killed by falling trees (James Bruce, Rufus Atwater, Tom Jones, and William MacIntosh). Four others froze to death (John Fitzpatrick, Daniel Bigsby, John Wood and Daniel Conner). Being bordered by water and frequently employed on the sea, drowning was common. It was how early residents travelled and where they found much of their diet. In fact the first section of the Antigonish Guysborough Road was over water from Guysborough to the Crossroads at the Intervale. A land road to the Intervale wasn't completed until around 1840. There were 15 individuals listed as having drowned. They included William Nixon Jr., the son of an early entrepreneur, and father and daughter Robert and Abigail Till. Of the 15 listed, Abigail was the only female. One individual, Conrad Fletcher, was lost at sea, and four months later the priest of the day stated "his half-mangled corpse washed ashore."

Finally, there were three unusual burial entries. Ithiel Hart was killed by lightning, Alexander Tory "drank too much rum" and finally there is Mary Nocton (aged 20) who was refused burial in St. Anne's Roman Catholic cemetery in June of 1870. Shortly after, a John Nocton was also referenced in the burial list.

Tombstones Visible in 1921

by Duncan Floyd, K. C. (From a 1921 copy of the Canso Breeze)

Among the stones still standing in Christ Church Cemetery, Guysboro, is that of Elias Cook, one of the nine old settlers at Cook's Cove. He died on March 10, 1809 at the age of eighty eight years. On the 18th of February 1833 a son of Elias, Benjamin, died and is buried here. He was 65 years old. His wife, Philo died May 13th, 1809.

There are some names that have completely died out. Among them may be mentioned that of William R. Cantrell, M. D. "A native of Waterford, Ireland, and who died at Guysborough in Oct. 1839 aged 47 years." Another name not familiar is that of Mettzler, Charles R. Mettzler, M. D. Died at Guysboro, Dec. 15, 1870. Benjamin Elliott died Dec. 6, 1846, and Elizabeth his wife on Nov. 6, 1835. William Nixon died on March 21, 1801 aged 53 years. Other names with the dates of death are as follows;

W.J. Pomeroy Mattocks, Jan. 20, 1871
Hon. Robert M. Cutler, May 1, 1890
Francis Marla Pearl, aug. 8, 1859
Thomas C. Peart, Jan. 29, 1881
Peter Frost, Aug. 18, 1828
Louise Sophia Clarke, Beg. 21, 1820
George McMaster, June 1, 1838
Tiras Hart, July 7, 1828
Martha Hart, May 15, 1820
Henry Carr, dec. 10, 1868
Annie Welsh, June 2, 1804
Isaac Wylde, Nov. 19, 1837
Wylde came from Oldham, Lancashire, England and was 47 years old at the time of his death.
Edward Carritte, M. D., Oct. 11, 1888
Harriet Carritte, Jan. 26, 1884
Edmund H. Francheville, 1876
Sarah E. Francheville, 1903

James Shaw, Jan. 3, 1858
Patrick Patton, June 9, 1816
Godfrey S. Peart, March 10, 1884
Martha R. Peart, Aug. 16, 1881
Edward Mollison, Sept. 27, 1787
Esther Hadley, Oct. 14, 1807
Harriet Ann Shreve, March 13, 1851

Christ Church Graveyard List

1787
Ann Farfer   16 days
William Atwater   53
Charlotte Cowen   21
Charles Morgan   25
John MacKenzie 5 m.
Henry Scranton   14

1788
Daniel Bigsby   63
James Lenox   24
Patience Ward   80
Edward Morris   3
William Frazer   28
Ann McDougle   1 m.
John Wood   32

1789
Simon Ash   3 m.
Conrad Fletcher   43
William Nixon   11
Marianne Hulme 5 m.
John Merriman 16 m.

1790
John Hansel   30
Rufus Atwater   35
Sarah Stuart   30
Alexander Tory   44
William Steward   51
Ruth Hadley   66
Mathea Godfrey   20

1791
Charles Gilly   10
Hannah Luddington 21
Mary Gilly   5
Mary Farfer   2
Ann Cogill   5
Robert Till   36
Abigail Till   15
Hannah Hanline   2
Ann DeLaRoche   52
Henry Heule
ames Patte   7 wks
Bridget Fitzpatrick 3 m.
Diziah Tobin   14 m.

1792
Ann Bolton   23
Malachi Jones   33

George Bedford   3
David Patten   3 wks

1793
Elspeth McKay   5 m.
Elizabeth Nixon   9
Ann Nixon   6
Amelia Thetford   20
James Shaw   20 m.

1794
William Warrington 3 m

1795
Rev. Peter De La Roche 63

1796
Unknown Soldier
James Taylor
girl McKay   9

1797
Elias Cook   52
Gap in available records:
1798 – 1803

1804
George Henline
child Dickoff
Bulia Scranton   13
William Nixon   55
John Davis
William Grant   55
Isabella Shaw
John Peart   39
Chris Whitendale   25
William Roberts   3
Elizabeth Murphy   11
Jane Murphy   3
Submit Leet   50
David Connor   45
William McIntosh   51
William Wallbrecht 57

1805
Robert Dorrington
James Moore
Abigail Partridge 9 days
Ann Welsh   35
Miss Hurly   50
Foster Thetford   14

1806
James Bruce   40
Mary Strople   60

Benjamin Godfrey   67
John Pringle   67
Duncan McArthur very old
Mary Warrington   40
Laura Scranton

1807
Christine Torey   60
Catherine Redding 70
William David   62
Elizabeth Munro   29
James Bundy   55
Esther Hadley   72
Murdock Campbel 49
Dinah ?   85
Edmond Heffernan40
Ithiel Hart   24
eter Sellars   2 m.

1808
Child MacIntyre 1 day
Alexander Gardner   6 m.
Elizabeth Anderson 9 m.
John Fitzpatrick   88
Andrew Leet   79
Margaret Erskine   7
regory Martin   ??
Cameron   68

1809
Elias Cook   88
Elizabeth Kirby   1
Philomela Cook   40
Alexander Imlay   1
ohn Hamilton   50
Edward McAtfray   60
John Gardner   49
John Gilly   18
ydia Hart   73

1810
Henry Partridge   2
William Peart   20 m.
Abigail Bayard
nn Evans   70
hild Dorrington
Gaseha Dickhoff   2 m.
George MacKenzie   2
oseph Stringer   16 m.
John Maglees

Sam Wilson 60
Mary Wheaton 83
Christian Schneider
1811
Thomas Hilton 25
u/k woman 30
Foster Sherlock 62
Duncan McCallm 25
George Klasgye 9 m.
John Shanaway
James Roberts
enry Morgan 2
1812
?? Whitford 80
Malcom McCallum
Anna Cook
Mary Spanks
Elizabeth Dorrington
Evan Shaw
Stephan Bears 6
James McGill 60
George MacMaster 1
Catherine Kirby 4 m.
Lydia Hart 12 days
Robert Hartshorne
1813
Jane Stewart 17 days
Benjamin Baker 16
James Imlay 50
Margart Baker
ohn Shaw
James Pyle 10
Mary Campbell 4
George Whitman 1
girl Hadley 13
William Green 40
Ann Ross
1814
James Stewart 16
Esther Whitman 42
eter Cummings
Frances Irvine
Jabez Leet 37
Alexander Ferguson 56
annah Hawkins
1815
Michael Willis 2 m.
John Creshine
Hugh Hugh
eorge Strople

Joseph Coates
Elizabeth Aiken
Donald Cogill 60
Jared Luddington 40
1816
Nelson Ballaine 13
Susanna Lucas 54
Joseph Marshall 32
Elizabeth Tobey 95
Thomas Brown 20
Sophia MacDonald 51
Patrick Patton 64
James MacDonald 70
Margaret Morris 3
Margaret Taylor 7 m.
Aaron Brown 70
Henry Jones 67
1817
Mary Nockton 11
Thomas Dillon 1 day
George Grant 3 m.
Sarah Weeks 80
George Whitman 20
Charles Marsh 3 m.
William Lawson 58
Thomas Combes 60
Conrad Demus
James Grant
1818
Sarah Cosins 1
James McKay
Mathew Welsh
Alice Creamer
Elizabeth Atwater 31
Benjamin Godfrey
Elizabeth Elliot
David Crowdis
Frances Gilly 60
James Harrel
Richard Anderson 30
Betsy Elliott
Alexander Cummings
1819
Elizabeth Wilson 80
Thomas Morris
Ann Nixon 70
James Grant 7 m.
James Keay
Mary Wilson 21

Christian Whitman 3 days
1820
?? Wilson
Margaret Marshall 72
Martha Hart 72
Christie Morris 11
Frederick Weeks 1 day
1821
Isabella Bears 4
Alexander Grant 13 days
?? Gilly 66
Hannah Harris
Elizabeth McKenzie 1
Robert Pearson
Charles Roberts 7
1822
Jane. McCallum 79
James Kent
Mathias Irvine
Henry Warrington 60
?? Cameron
Eleanor Davidson
James Cummings 1
?? Shaw
William Scott 28
?? Whitman 1
Thomas Anderson 32
Ebenezer Partridge 5
Francis Cook
Henry Morgan
John Torey
?? Torey
Hibbert McPherson 2
?? McGregor 3
1823
Mrs. Carr 9?
Robert Carr 67
Moses Cook 1
Jane Ryan 38
Mary McPherson 2
?? Cook
Abraham Whitman
Mrs. Fitzpatrick
James Bear
Mrs. Sherlock
William Gray 36
Abijah Scott
? Fitzpatrick
1824
Anthony Peacock 42

George Weeks   23
1825
James Tarbot
girl Johnson
Ann Whitman
Margery Aikens
Mary Foster   53
John Sellars   9
James Harris   30
Phobe Whitman
Samual Aikens
Donald Glen   2 m.
1826
? Lipsit
Martha Hart   44
Cassandra Miller
Ann Roberston   43
Mary Cummings   13 days
1827
Sukey Tarbot
William Gillie   33
Isaac Harty   6 m.
John Petterson   40
James Aikens
Alexander McKay   16 m.
Daniel Harrington
Hugh Hastic
Malcolm McColl
Sarah Harrington
Catherine Bush   97
Harriet Peart   5
Peter Bayard
Alexander Rattray   47
Christina Morris   1 m.
1828
William Glen   17
Abijah Scott
Abigail Johnson
Robert McColl
May Shaw   67
Paul McPherson   94
Ann Butler   54
Mrs. Gunn   94
Tyrus Hart   54
Peter Frost   49
?? Mercer   80
Richard Rundle
1829
Alexander Shaw
Henry Inch

James Luca   80
George Bears   2
Robert ?   9 m.
Mary Glen
Moses Pyle   22
John Greshin
Maria Peart   32
?? McPherson
Levi Whitman
William Cantrell   47
?? Hadley
?? Jeffrey
1830
Charles Weeks Jr.
Harold Roberts
Stephan Field   68
Jeanette Davidso   14
Rufus Whitman
John Grant
Martha Lawson
Charles McPherson
Elizabeth McColl   8
John Malachi   1 m.
Mary Cummings   40
Francis Featherston
William Johnson   33
1831
Joshua Caldwell   20
Wallace McColl   15 days
Cynthia Morris   63
Sarah Ringwood
?? Mina
Godfrey Peart
John Bond
Alexander Mortimer
John Gunn
John McPherson
Elizabeth Dickoff
1832
Ann McMaster
Mary. Pearson   91
Jane Mortimer
?? Morris   1
Christopher Morris 17
?? Lawrence
Cynthia Imlay   4
Alexander Brown
Sarah Weeks   21
lizabeth Cutler   67

1833
Kenneth McKenzie 33
William Foster   85
Benjamin Cook   68
Margaret Patton
Henry Torrey   11 m.
George Stropel   50
Mrs. McDonald
argaret Greshine   51
James Foster   25
1834
Margaret Aikens   40
Jane Patterson
1835
Elizabeth Elliot   69
1836
Catherine Emily   4
Jane Anderson   32
James Bowie   85
Alvarus Atwater   18
Sarah Hue
Simon MacKenzie   3
John Wilson   51
Priscilla Tory   17
1837
Mary Willis   85
ames Davidson   6
William Cantrill
John Gritney   26
Thomas Cutler   5
Joseph Wheaton   68
Titus Luddington   89
Elizabeth Russell   5
Isaac Wylde   48
Christiann McKay 75
ubmit Partridge   65
1838
George MacMaster49
Jane Hall79
Jane Campbell   48
Joseph Hadley   82
Alexander Carr   7 m.
Henry Creamer   80
Ann Campbell   32
Eleanor Hadley   7
1839
Agnus Shreve,, 6 days
Herman Dickoff   88
Barbara MacPherso 47
John Snider   35

152

Jacob Anderson
Mary Armsworthy 20
Samuel Jefferies
Peter Lawrence 92
J. McMaster 82
Harriet Grady 49
Peter Roberts 68
Elizabeth Mintus 5 wks
Robert Grant 8 wks
Maria Wylde 15
Allison Porter 68
John Byard
?? McKenzie

1840

Thomas Hall 90
Andrew Mintus
Duncan McMaster 40
John Cook 88
Robert Grant 1
John Carr 11
May Carr 81
Stephan Pile 80
Sarah Morris 14
George Wentzell 43
Mary Grant 58
James MacPherson 11
Charles Myers 75

1841

Christian Mueller 90
Bridget O'Brien 60
James Graham 2
Ann Dorrington 14
Joseph Williams 5
Dougle Cummings 36
Jarret Hues 32

1842

John Jamieson 81
Cynthia Grant 56
Sarah MacPherson 3 wks
Samuel Giles 54
Elsie Shields, 8 m.
Ann Imlay 9 m.
Margaret Atwater 18
Susan Butterworth 26
Sarah Peart 88
James Leet
John Carrigan 6
Thomas Anderson 97
James Gritney 24

1843

James Keay 45
Edmund Twiford 69
John Dorrington 80
Alexander Grant 72
Sarah Sellars 4
Elizabeth Cook 61
Lydia Byard about 50
Hannah McKenzie 79

1844

Mary Anderson 57
? O Brien
Amelia Lawrence 72
Elizabeth Nash 80
Annie Foster 12
John MacIntosh 47
Godfrey Wheaton 30

1845

Nancy Reed 24
John Foster 51
Mary Anderson 87
Anthony Siles 80
Sarah Atwater 87
James Dismil 60
Henrietta Francheville 10 m.
William Jeffers 70
Catherine Hooper 62
Ann Lipsett 5
William Davidson 10 m.

1846

Grace Keay 96
Elizabeth Dixon 6
W. Atwater 82
Ann Mueller 82
Edward Cook 94
Benjamin Elliott 93

1847

Harriet Hartshorne 60
Robert Simpson 8
Lydia Henderson 50
Colin Porter 72
Charlotte S. 4
George Whitman 80
James Sellars 32
Mary Ann Morris 24
James McCallum 59
William Morris 11
Donald Grant 55
Cynthia Roberts 42
Harriet Roberts 2 m.

Robert Hartshorne 4 m
Eliza Carter 6

1848

Maria DesBarres 14
Richard Carter 77
Mary MacPherson 90
Mary Cochran 37
William Wilson 56
Theodore Cochran 12 days
Mary Willis 54
James McVie? 75
Mary Greencorn 88
Margaret MacMaster 47
Henry Lamb 3
Alexander Gritney
John Johnston 45
Margaret Sellars 72
Joseph Marshall 93
John March 74
Edmond Mountain 57
Donald Sellars 90
William Glenn 15
Isabel Clark 29
Catherine Strople 37
Rebecca Devost 6 m.
Jeremiah Byard 1

1849

Lydia Luddington 87
Lydia Wheaton 73
Elizabeth Grove 6 m.
Fredrick Greencorn 40
William McLaughlin 2
George Whitman 90
Margaret Keay 22
Lois MacMaster

1850

Asa MacKenzie 4
Ann Lipsett 12
Malcolm Sellars 6
William Byard 47
Robert Kay 81
John Campbell
Sophia Cutler 58
Hugh Miller 91
Robert Carr 27

1851

Thomas Byard 1
Thomas Morris 40
Harriet Shreve 34 ?
Robert Hartshorne 77

James Harris   94
Edward Morrimer   7
Peter Lawrence   52
Margaret Lawrence 64
Susan Johnston about 80
Charles Grant   4
George Francheville 4
1852
Catherine Dickoff   18
Robert Johnston   18
Ann MacKenzie   16
Marjory Cummings 90
Submit Grant   8 m.
Warburton Campbell 87
Peter Johnston   14
Marjory Wilson   52
Mary Johnston   11
Alexander Peart 6 wks
1853
George Imlay   41
Ellen Aiken   12
John Hyde   70
John Hyde   45
1854
Ida Clark   6
David Griffin   62
Thomas Shields ? 53
Joseph Hadley   69
Mary Ann Carr
Mrs. Irvin
Sarah Hyde   72
1855
Margaret Willis
Samuel Aiken   65
James Grady   86
Ann Foster   12
Thomas Fraser   6 m.
1856
Caroline McColl   64
John Peart   69
Helen Wilson   3 m.
Jane Irving   54
Margaret Reid   56
Ellen McCall   23
June Armsworthy 19
Phoebe Sceles   85
Dorothy Williams 40
1857
Alexander MacMaster 38
James Johnston   90

Sarah Wilson   34
Edward Lipset   63
John Bolt
May ?   77
Catherine Dort   38
John Greencorn   65
Jessy James Reid 36
Louisa Wylde   23
John Hurst   76
Jacob Anderson   23
John Fraser   79
Helen Jarvis   7 wks
Emma Grant   2
1858
James Shaw   64
Michael Gritney   31
Jane Wilson   22
George Griffin   22
Hannah Creshin   92
William Grant   2
Angus McKay   69
Hugh Cummings   64
Margaret Irvin   65
Eliza Anne Keay   25
William Jarvis   3 wks
Sarah McKenzie   15

1859
Ada Peart   26
James Johns   90
Harriet Dorrington 6
Thomas Byard   14 m.
Frances Peart   19
1860
Mary Jarvis   4 wks
Valentine Dort   39
Dorothy Horton   67
Elias Foster   24
Albert Peart   4 m.
1861
Mary Gritney   75
1862
John Cogill   70
Thomas Peart   22
1863
Harriet Byard   3
1864
Thomas L Peart   24
1865
Mary Carritte   2

Sarah MacMaster 78
Murdock McLean 58
Elizabeth Tore   45
Jane Richardson   23
Francis Cutler   1
James Porper   30
John Appleton   11
1866
Andrew Willis   64
John McDonald   76
1867
Frederick DesBarres
Alfred Francheville 27
oseph Francheville 26
1868
Thomas Peart   82
child Peart
Henry Carr   61
1869
Charlotte Dorrington 56
Mary Peart   78
William Delaney   30
Margaret McDonald 84
1870
Louisa Clark
Daniel Aikens   82
Mary Nocton   20
David Nocton   7
Mary MacDonald
Stewart Peart   26
William Shaw   82
Charles Metzler   33
Thomas Brownspriggs 92
1871
William Mattocks 91
Joseph Jamieson
Cathy Dorrington 74
1872
John McMaster   52
Marjory Kay
1873-1874: No burials recorded
1875
Murdock Campbell 40
Samuel Russell   67
Arthur Appleton   23
1876
Edward Cutler   18
George McMaster 7
Hugh Cougle   23

154

Janet Delany
Edmund Franchville 66
James Imlay   72
1877
James Marshall   68
Asa MacKenzie   87
Mrs. Asa MacKenzie 80
Henry Williams   86
1878
George MacKridge 10 hrs
Marjory Carr   75
1879
Samuel Byard   69
Elizaabeth Tory   82
Maria Carritte   48
James Carr   28
Edward Nocton   60
David Sellers   71
1880
William Hadley   36
1881
Thomas Peart   67
Martha Peart   70
Jarius Imlay   17 days
1882
James Imlay   28
1883
John Appleton   70
Elizabeth Foster   71
Jarius   76
Robert Cutler   98
Esther Gosbee   82
1884
Harriet Carritte   77
Mary Imlay   6 m.
Godfrey Peart   73
Violet Schaffner   1
1885
Lydia MacPherson 36
1886
Georgina Campbell 70
Eugenia Francheville 25
1887
John Irvine   18
1888
John Peart   35
Edward Carritte   88
Sadie Francheville 35
1889
Esther Peart   27

Amelia Hartley   18
Mary Eaton   95
1890
Mrs. Jarius Campbell 91
Ann Grant   75
Jarius Campbell   92
1891
James Tory   68
1892 – 1893: No burials recorded
1894
Florence Byard   1
Thomas Carritte   10
1896
George Byard   1 day
1897
Mary Hadley   1 day
1899
Lavinia Skinner   88
Josiah Hull   62
1900
Lois Peart   1 day
1902
Frances Peart   89
1903
William Carritte   74
Sarah Francheville 84
1904
Mary Reade   86
William Skinner   77
1905-1908: No burials recorded
1909
Annie Carritte   74
Robert Kay   85
1910
Henrietta Martin 75
1911 – 1915: No burials recorded
1916
William Hyde   80
1917-1918: No burials recorded
1919
Eliza Tory   91
1920
Kenneth Horton   49 days
Moses Foster   71
J Jones   81

1921-1923: No burials recorded
1924
Joseph Lee Martin   91
1925
Sarah Snider   60
1926
Levi Pelley   68
1927
Isaac Dorrington   47
1929
Douglas Pelley   1
1930
Ida Russell   75
Lucy Pelley   4
Sarah Campbell   85
Abigail Merrick   79
Mary Bixbee   95
1931
Austin Berg   51
1933
William Irving   33
Wilfred Dort   38
1934
Annie White   71
Louise Pelley   32
1936
Gertrude Clyke   4 m.
Stewart Peart   83
1938
Frank Merrick   82
No Years Given
Helen Tate   3
Alexander Ferguson

www.ingramcontent.com/pod-product-compliance
Lightning Source LLC
LaVergne TN
LVHW011353080426

835511LV00005B/262